125 Best
Chicken
Recipes

125 Best Chicken Recipes

Rose Murray

Robert
ROSE

For complete cataloguing information, see page 6.

Originally published in 1999 as *Quick Chicken*.

Disclaimer
The recipes in this book have been carefully tested by our kitchen and our tasters. To the
best of our knowledge, they are safe and nutritious for ordinary use and users. For those
people with food or other allergies, or who have special food requirements or health
issues, please read the suggested contents of each recipe carefully and determine whether
or not they may create a problem for you. All recipes are used at the risk of the consumer.

We cannot be responsible for any hazards, loss or damage that may occur as a result of
any recipe use.

For those with special needs, allergies, requirements or health problems, in the event
of any doubt, please contact your medical adviser prior to the use of any recipe.

Cover design and art direction: PageWave Graphics Inc.
Design, editorial and production: Matthews Communications Design Inc.
Photography: Mark T. Shapiro
Art direction/food photography: Sharon Matthews
Food stylist: Kate Bush
Prop stylist: Charlene Erricson
Managing editor: Peter Matthews
Test kitchen: Lesleigh Landry and Jan Main
Indexer: Barbara Schon
Color scans & film: PointOne Graphics

Cover Image: Easy Chicken and Vegetable Stir-Fry (see recipe, page 24)

We acknowledge the financial support of the Government of Canada through the Book
Publishing Industry Development Program (BPIDP) for our publishing activities.

Published by: Robert Rose Inc.
120 Eglinton Ave. E., Suite 800, Toronto, Ontario, Canada M4P 1E2
Tel: (416) 322-6552 Fax: (416) 322-6936

Printed in Canada
1 2 3 4 5 6 7 GP 09 08 07 06 05 04 03

Contents

National Library of Canada Cataloguing in Publication

Murray, Rose, 1941-
    125 best chicken recipes / Rose Murray.

Previously published under title: Quick chicken.

Includes index.
ISBN 0-7788-0069-5

1. Cookery (Chicken). 2. Quick and easy cookery. I. Title.
II. Title: One hundred twenty-five best chicken recipes.

TX750.5.C45M87 2003   641.6'65   C2003-901331-6

Photo Prop Credits

The publisher and authors wish to express their appreciation to the following supplier of props used in the food photography appearing in this book:

Dishes, cutlery, glassware, linens and accessories   IKEA CANADA

Introduction

When you meet an acquaintance on the street today, a simple "How're you doing?" is typically answered with something like "I've been so busy."

Our lives just get busier and busier, but families still need three meals a day. Somehow breakfasts and lunches are fairly easy to handle: there's plenty of choice in convenience foods such as cereals, fresh fruit and breads with their endless variety of fillings.

But it's the evening meal that's the hardest. Everyone is tired, and the kids are hungry. Or, you decide to invite a couple of friends over after work. It's at times like these that supper cooked in under 30 minutes has great appeal.

But why chicken? Well, judging from the amount of space chicken occupies in the supermarket, everyone certainly seems to like it. What's more, chicken lends itself perfectly to a quick-cooking theme. Since it's already tender, it doesn't need a long simmering to make it palatable.

Chicken is also an extremely versatile food: you can serve it several times a week, and in such different ways that it's like a whole new food each time. One night it can be popped into the oven for a quick roast, perhaps with a glaze or some vegetables alongside. Another time, it can be part of a one-pot skillet supper on top of the stove. The various parts of a chicken also provide different personalities — crunchy wings, silky smooth pan-fried boneless breasts, succulent thighs with crisp skin, and hearty ground chicken for burgers.

Add a few ingredients to it and chicken also happily takes up flavors from around the world. With chicken you can travel to all corners of the globe — to the Orient for quick stir-fries, Europe for an updated Coq au Vin or Saltimbocca, India for the savory curry flavors of Easy Tandoori, the Southwest for Tex-Mex Wings, Mexico for juicy Roasted Chicken Fajitas, or the Middle East for a wonderful Moroccan Baked Chicken. It's easy to see that cooks around the world have always appreciated the goodness and versatility of chicken.

Chicken is there for you in summer to sizzle on the barbecue or join fresh fruit or vegetables in a refreshing salad. It's warming against winter chills in hearty soups and skillet stews. When company's coming, it can be dressed in its luscious best. Yet it's still great in everyday foods like spaghetti sauce or on a pizza for fast, weeknight family meals.

After busy days, when your family is hungry, I hope you come to rely on these recipes for suppers that take less time than ordering in.

— *Rose Murray*

The Quick Chicken Pantry

Besides essentials like flour, sugar, eggs, butter, milk and bread, it pays to have a few other ingredients on hand for quick meals. I always have a hunk of real Parmesan cheese (which keeps for ages ready to be grated when I need it), a good-size chunk of fresh ginger, condiments (my staples include Tabasco sauce, soya sauce, Dijon mustard and Worcestershire sauce), fresh garlic, fresh lemons, cans of chicken broth, rice, oils, vinegars and a vast selection of herbs and spices on hand.

The following is a list of handy ingredients to have on hand to make the quick recipes in this book:

IN THE CUPBOARD

Asian ingredients. These include coconut milk, oyster sauce, sesame oil, hoisin sauce, fish sauce and chili paste; with the exception of the latter two (for which you may have to go to an Asian market), these ingredients are all widely available in supermarkets.

Beans. The more types, the better — kidney, white, chickpeas, lentils, and so on.

Bread crumbs (dried) and **cornmeal.** Good for coating chicken.

Canned chicken broth. Useful for recipes calling for small amounts of stock, where homemade is not so important. Instant stock powder can also be used.

Cornstarch. An essential thickening agent.

Condiments and sauces. Basics include ketchup, mango chutney, Tabasco, soya sauce (preferably the low-salt variety) and Worcestershire sauce. Keep in the refrigerator after opening.

Garlic and onions. Essential for any type of cooking.

Herbs and spices. A good variety of spices and dried herbs, especially Italian herb seasoning, thyme, hot pepper flakes, oregano, and cumin.

Honey. The liquid variety is most useful for cooking.

Mustard. Staple varieties include Dijon, regular prepared and dry mustard.

Oil. Keep a good-quality olive oil and vegetable oil on hand.

Pasta and noodles. Keep a good variety of dried pasta and noodles on hand.

Pasta sauce. Meatless spaghetti sauce is the most versatile.

Peanut butter. If you've got kids, chances are it's already in the cupboard.

Red peppers. Keep a jar of roasted red peppers (packed in water) on hand.

Rice and couscous. Both are good as accompaniments to chicken dishes.

Salsa. Keep a bottle of prepared salsa (mild or hot — or both) on the shelf; refrigerate after opening.

Tomatoes. Stock up on several sizes of *canned tomatoes* (now available in a variety of types — crushed, diced, whole or stewed), *tomato sauce* and *tomato paste* (most supermarkets now sell this in tubes), as well as *sun-dried tomatoes* (dry ones are less expensive and can be rehydrated in warm water; they can then be packed in oil if you wish).

Vinegar. White, cider, rice, wine and balsamic varieties are all useful.

REFRIGERATOR AND FREEZER STAPLES

Citrus fruits. Essentials include lemons, limes and oranges.

Cheese. *Parmesan* and *Cheddar* are the varieties most often used in recipes.

Frozen vegetables. Peas, corn and Oriental vegetables are good.

Mayonnaise. Always useful.

Parsley. Keep the fresh type on hand.

Nuts and sesame seeds. Should be refrigerated to keep from going rancid.

Yogurt and sour cream. Apart from milk, the most often-used dairy ingredients.

If you're missing an ingredient...

In many cases, a missing ingredient can be replaced by another. Here's a useful list of ingredients and their possible substitutes:

Balsamic vinegar. For 1/4 cup (50 mL) balsamic vinegar, use 3 tbsp (45 mL) red wine vinegar plus 1/4 tsp (1 mL) granulated sugar

Buttermilk. Stir together 1 tbsp (15 mL) lemon juice or vinegar with enough sweet milk to makes 1 cup (250 mL).

Cheese. For *mozzarella*, Provolone is a flavorful substitute; for *Swiss*, try Fontina; and for *Parmesan*, Asiago or Romano are both good.

Chicken stock. In recipes calling for large amounts of stock, the homemade variety is clearly the best. (See EASY CHICKEN BROTH recipe, page 14.) Canned broth will do in a pinch. Use instant stock mixes only as a last resort since they are usually very high in salt and often contain MSG.

Chorizo. Use pepperoni or other spicy sausage.

Pasta. You can usually interchange any type of pasta for another, since the recipe choice often depends on shape; however, corkscrew or bow-tie pastas will collect sauce better in a dish.

Shallots. Use mild onion and a bit of garlic.

Chicken Essentials

While a well-stocked pantry is important for preparing the recipes in this book, it's the chicken that really matters. Here's my advice on buying, storing and cooking your chicken.

BUYING

Always check the best-before date on the package when buying chicken from the supermarket. Check that there's not too much water in the package or red spots on the chicken (these are a sign of bruising). Air-chilled chicken is best, but not always available.

STORING

Place the chicken package on a tray or plate and store in the coldest part of the refrigerator — the temperature should be about 40° F (4° C) — placing it so that no liquid from the chicken drips onto other foods. If the chicken is not being cooked the same day, remove it from the package, place on a clean plate and wrap with waxed paper or clean plastic wrap. Before storing, rinse chicken and pat dry.

In the refrigerator, store whole chicken and chicken pieces no longer than 2 to 3 days, ground chicken for no longer than 1 day, and cooked chicken up to 3 days.

For longer storage, freeze chicken by wrapping it well in an airtight freezer bag. Keep whole chickens no longer than 12 months (if well wrapped and your freezer is good), chicken pieces no longer than 6 months, and cooked chicken up to 3 months.

Frozen chicken should never be thawed at room temperature. Allow 5 hours per 1 lb (500 g) in the refrigerator. You can thaw chicken in sealed packages in cold water, changing the water often and allowing 1 hour per 1 lb (500 g). In the microwave, thaw on Defrost setting, separating and turning the pieces as the chicken thaws and allowing 5 minutes per 1 lb (500 g). Refrigerate thawed chicken immediately and cook within 2 days. Never refreeze thawed chicken.

COOKING

Be sure to cook chicken long enough, although overcooking will often dry it out, especially boneless breasts. Check often around the time suggested. Chicken is cooked when it is no longer pink inside at its thickest part and with whole legs, thighs or drumsticks, when juices run clear as they are pierced with a fork at the thickest part. To be on the safe side too, wash your hands with soap and warm water before and after handling raw chicken. Always thoroughly wash any equipment, boards, knives and the like after it has seen raw chicken. To be really safe, wash any equipment with a solution of 1 part bleach to 4 parts water. Never put cooked chicken on the unwashed surface of the raw.

ON THE GRILL

Use tongs to turn chicken so that there's no piercing to allow juices to run out.

Brush on very sweet glazes only in the last 5 or 10 minutes of grilling to avoid burning.

If you use a marinade that held the raw chicken for brushing on as the chicken cooks, be sure the chicken continues to cook for at least 5 minutes after the last brush to allow the marinade to cook thoroughly.

If basting brushes used on the raw or partly cooked chicken are dipped into a sauce or marinade and you want to serve the sauce with the chicken, boil it for 2 minutes before serving. Always use a clean plate to take cooked chicken off the grill. Never put it on the same plate that held it raw. Remember that barbecue times are variable according to the outside temperature, wind, type of barbecue and so on; cut into chicken to check for doneness and don't rely only on time given.

A WORD ABOUT CHICKEN BREASTS

Please note: Throughout this book, any chicken breast called for in a recipe is a single breast half — not a double, whole breast.

Easy Chicken Broth

**MAKES ABOUT
11 CUPS (2.75 L)**

A good broth or stock makes a good soup. If it's too salty or weak, the soup will quickly reflect these flaws. Obviously, a good homemade broth is the best and not difficult to make. When you are home for a few hours, put a pot on the stove, cool and freeze containers for future use. If time or mood doesn't allow you to make your own, however, the next best bet is canned broth.

3 lbs	meaty chicken bones (necks, wings, backs)	1.5 kg
1	unpeeled onion, cut into chunks	1
1	unpeeled carrot, cut into chunks	1
2	stalks celery, cut into chunks	2
1	large fresh tomato, coarsely chopped or 2 canned tomatoes, chopped	1
4	sprigs parsley	4
1	bay leaf	1
Pinch	thyme	Pinch
1 1/2 tsp	salt, preferably coarse pickling type	7 mL

1. Place bones, onion, carrot, celery, tomato, parsley, bay leaf, thyme and salt in a large kettle or stockpot. Pour in 16 cups (4 L) cold water and slowly bring to a boil, skimming any solids that rise to the surface. Reduce heat and simmer gently, uncovered, for 5 to 6 hours or until rich broth develops.

2. Strain through a fine sieve into a large bowl, pushing hard on solids. Discard solids and let broth cool. Refrigerate, covered, for up to 2 days or freeze for up to 6 months. Before using or freezing broth, remove fat from top.

Basic Whole Roast Chicken

Leftovers from a Sunday roast chicken provide the basis for many quick and wonderful dishes throughout the week — so much so that you might even want to roast two chickens, one for Sunday and one for other days. Of course, you can roast chickens smaller than called for here (anything from about 3 1/2 lbs (1.75 kg) and up is fine); just adjust the time, allowing 20 to 30 minutes per pound (500 g).

PREHEAT OVEN TO 325° F (160° C)

1	roasting chicken (about 5 lbs [2.5 kg])	1
Half	lemon	Half
	Salt and pepper	
1	onion, quartered	1
1 tbsp	butter, softened	15 mL
1 tbsp	Dijon mustard	15 mL
1/2 tsp	dried thyme	2 mL
1/2 tsp	crushed dried sage	2 mL

1. Remove giblets and neck from chicken. Rinse and pat dry inside and out; rub inside and out with lemon. Sprinkle inside and out with salt and pepper. Place onion in cavity. Tie legs together with string; tuck wings under back. Place, breast side up, on rack in roasting pan.

2. Combine butter, mustard, thyme and sage; spread over chicken. Roast in preheated oven for about 2 hours or until juices run clear when chicken is pierced and a meat thermometer inserted in the thigh registers 185° F (85° C).

3. Transfer chicken to a platter; tent with foil and let stand for 10 to 15 minutes before carving for juices to settle into meat.

Woks, Wings and Wraps

Burmese Chicken Thighs

This simple dish is loaded with flavor.

I've discovered bottled lemon grass in my local supermarket where fresh lemon grass is not always available. If you have fresh, use only the bottom 6 inches (15 cm) of the stalk, trimming off the root end and straw-like top. Cut into lengths and crush slightly with a chef's knife or mallet. Boneless thighs are available in most supermarkets.

1 tbsp	vegetable oil	15 mL
4	boneless chicken thighs, patted dry	4
2	onions, sliced	2
2	cloves garlic, minced	2
3	pieces (each 2 inches [5 cm]) lemon grass, crushed	3
1 tbsp	minced ginger root	15 mL
1/4 cup	water (approximate)	50 mL
2 tsp	curry powder	10 mL
2 tbsp	soya sauce	25 mL

1. In a wok heat oil over high heat. Add the chicken and cook until browned on both sides. Remove with a slotted spoon.

2. Add onions to wok; reduce the heat to medium–high and stir-fry for 3 minutes. Add the garlic, lemon grass and ginger; stir-fry for 1 minute, adding water if the mixture sticks. Stir in curry powder; cook for 1 minute. Stir in the soya sauce and add the chicken back, along with any juice. Cover and simmer for 10 to 12 minutes or until the chicken is no longer pink inside. Remove and discard lemon grass.

★ *Honeyed Carrots*
Add liquid honey to taste to hot steamed carrot slices and sprinkle with chopped fresh coriander.

★ *Cucumber Salad*
Dress sliced cucumbers with rice vinegar, water, and a pinch each of granulated sugar and hot pepper flakes.

SUGGESTED MENU

Burmese Chicken Thighs

🐦

Rice

🐦

★ Honeyed Carrots

🐦

★ Cucumber Salad

🐦

Gingered Melon

Szechuan Chicken and Peanuts with Chili Peppers

SERVES 4

Szechuan vies with the Hunan province for the spiciest of Chinese regional cuisines. You can make this simple stir-fry hotter by adding more chili peppers if you wish; or reduce the heat by adding fewer.

SUGGESTED MENU

Szechuan Chicken and Peanuts with Chili Peppers

❧

★ Steamed Oriental Vegetables

❧

White Rice

❧

Orange Wedges

★ *You can stir-fry vegetables like bok choy, mushrooms and red pepper strips in a bit of oil; add a small amount of water, cover and steam until tender. Or purchase a good frozen Oriental vegetable mix and cook according to the package instructions.*

2	whole chicken breasts*, cut into 1/2-inch (1 cm) pieces	2
1 tbsp	minced ginger root	15 mL
2 tsp	light soya sauce	10 mL
1/4 tsp	salt	1 mL
1 tsp	cornstarch	5 mL
2 tbsp	peanut oil or vegetable oil	25 mL
1/2 cup	unsalted skinless peanuts	125 mL
4	small dried red chili peppers	4
1 tsp	rice vinegar	5 mL
1/2 tsp	granulated sugar	2 mL
	Boston or leaf lettuce leaves	

* *Chinese chefs usually bone the chicken breasts but leave the skin on before dicing. You can do the same or use 4 boneless skinless chicken breast halves.*

1. In a bowl combine the chicken, ginger, soya sauce, salt and cornstarch; set aside.

2. In a wok, heat oil over medium-high heat. Add peanuts and stir-fry for 2 minutes. Remove with a slotted spoon; set aside. Add chili peppers; stir-fry for 30 seconds. Remove with a slotted spoon and set aside. Add chicken mixture and stir-fry for 2 minutes. Add vinegar, sugar, reserved peanuts and chilies; cook for another 1 to 2 minutes.

3. Serve immediately on a lettuce-lined platter.

Stir-Fried Noodles with Chicken and Broccoli

SERVES 4

Have everything cut, measured and ready before you start stir-frying this one-dish supper.

SHOPPING TIPS

"Chow mein" means fried egg noodles, and this name will appear often on the package. Egg noodles are common in southern China and range in size from very fine strands to flat 1/4-inch (5 mm) ribbons. They may be purchased fresh, dried or fresh with oil. Some are dusted with a cornstarch-like coating; don't use this kind in recipes that call for stir-frying. Dried mushrooms, oyster sauce and chili paste may have to be purchased in an Oriental grocery store. Buy the chicken in stir-fry strips for quicker preparation.

1 lb	fresh thin Chinese egg noodles	500 g
1 tbsp	sesame oil	15 mL
1 tsp	salt	5 mL
1 lb	skinless boneless chicken breasts	500 g
4 tsp	cornstarch	20 mL
1 tbsp	rice wine or dry sherry	15 mL
8	medium Chinese dried black mushrooms	8
1 lb	broccoli (1 bunch or 2 or 3 heads)	500 g
1	large carrot, shredded	1
1/2 cup	chicken stock	125 mL
2 tbsp	soya sauce	25 mL
2 tbsp	oyster sauce	25 mL
1/2 tsp	granulated sugar	2 mL
4	cloves garlic, minced	4
1 tbsp	minced ginger root	15 mL
1 1/2 tsp	chili paste or chili sauce	7 mL
4 tbsp	peanut oil or vegetable oil	50 mL

1. In a colander fluff the noodles to undo any tangles. Add the noodles to a large pot of unsalted boiling water. Swish with a chopstick to separate the strands. Cook for 1 to 2 minutes or until tender but firm. Drain in a colander and refresh under cold running water; drain. Return the noodles to the cooking pot and toss with sesame oil and salt. Set aside.

2. Cut chicken across the grain in 1/8-inch (3 mm) strips. Toss with 1 tbsp (15 mL) of the cornstarch and the rice wine; set aside.

3. In a small bowl, soak the mushrooms in warm water to cover for at least 30 minutes and up to 1 hour. Drain, snip off the stems and cut into long slivers 1/8 inch (3 mm) wide.

4. Peel the stems of broccoli and cut crosswise on a diagonal into thin slices; cut the tops into small florets. Set aside with the carrot.

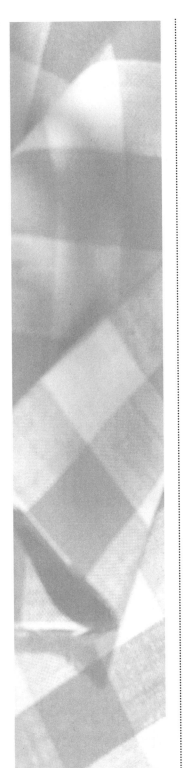

5. Dissolve the remaining 1 tsp (5 mL) cornstarch in 1 tbsp (15 mL) of chicken stock; set aside. Stir together remaining stock, soya sauce, oyster sauce and granulated sugar for the sauce; set aside. Set the garlic, ginger and chili paste to the side on a saucer.

6. In a very large wok, heat half the oil over high heat. Add garlic, ginger and chili paste; stir-fry for 10 seconds. Add chicken, broccoli, carrot and mushrooms; stir-fry for 3 minutes or until chicken is firm. Remove to a bowl.

7. Wipe out the wok. Heat remaining oil; add noodles and stir-fry until glazed with oil and heated through. Give sauce ingredients a stir and add to wok. Bring to a simmer, stirring. Stir cornstarch mixture and add, stirring until thickened, for about 20 seconds. Return the chicken and vegetables; toss to mix well and heat through. Serve immediately on a large heated platter.

SUGGESTED MENU

Stir-Fried Noodles with Chicken & Broccoli

🐦

Orange Sorbet & Fortune Cookies

Stir-Fried Chicken with Baby Corn and Snow Peas

There are lots of crunchy vegetables in this colorful stir-fry.

For convenience, look for chicken already cut into stir-fry strips.

1 lb	skinless boneless chicken breasts or thighs, cut into 1/4-inch (5 mm) strips	500 g
2 tbsp	soya sauce	25 mL
2 tbsp	rice wine *or* dry sherry	25 mL
1/2 tsp	pepper	2 mL
1 tbsp	rice vinegar	15 mL
1 tbsp	minced ginger root	15 mL
1	clove garlic, minced	1
1 tsp	cornstarch	5 mL
2 tbsp	peanut oil *or* vegetable oil	25 mL
4 oz	mushrooms, quartered	125 g
4 oz	snow peas, trimmed	125 g
1	red bell pepper, cut into strips	1
1/2 tsp	granulated sugar	2 mL
1	can (14 oz [398 mL]) whole baby corn, drained	1

1. Place chicken strips into a sturdy bag or bowl. Stir in half the soya sauce, half the wine and pepper. Let stand while preparing the remaining ingredients.

2. In another small bowl, stir together remaining soya sauce, wine, vinegar, ginger, garlic and cornstarch; set aside.

3. In a wok or large skillet, heat half the oil over high heat; stir-fry chicken for 3 minutes or until no longer pink inside. With a slotted spoon, remove to a warm platter and keep warm.

4. Heat remaining oil over high heat; stir-fry mushrooms for 1 minute. Add snow peas and red pepper; stir-fry for 1 minute. Stir in sugar, cover, and reduce heat to medium; cook for 30 seconds or until the vegetables are tender-crisp.

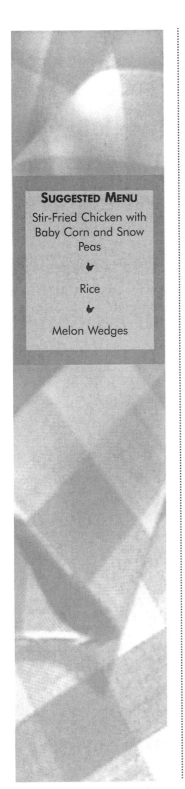

5. Uncover, increase heat to high and return the chicken; add corn. Pour soya-cornstarch mixture into the pan; cook, stirring constantly, for 1 minute or until the liquid is clear and thickened. Serve immediately.

Easy Chicken and Vegetable Stir-Fry

SERVES 2 OR 3

In supermarkets there are plenty of good frozen Oriental vegetables — all cut and ready to cook. They make this delicious stir-fry a breeze to prepare.

SUGGESTED MENU

Easy Chicken and
Vegetable Stir-Fry

Rice

Orange Wedges

2 tbsp	vegetable oil	25 mL
2	cloves garlic, minced	2
1 tbsp	minced ginger root	15 mL
1/4 tsp	hot pepper flakes, or to taste	1 mL
2	skinless boneless chicken breasts, cubed or cut into strips	2
1	pkg (12 oz [375 g]) frozen Oriental vegetables	1
1/2 cup	chicken stock	125 mL
2 tbsp	soya sauce	25 mL
2 tbsp	hoisin sauce	25 mL
2 tsp	cornstarch	10 mL
2 tsp	Oriental sesame oil	10 mL

1. In a large wok or heavy skillet, heat oil over high heat. Add garlic, ginger and hot pepper flakes; stir-fry for 30 seconds. Add chicken and stir-fry for about 3 minutes or until it changes color. Remove to a bowl with a slotted spoon.

2. Add vegetables to the wok; stir-fry for 1 minute. Pour in stock. Cover, reduce the heat and steam for 3 minutes or until vegetables are tender-crisp.

3. Meanwhile, in a small bowl, combine soya sauce, hoisin, cornstarch and sesame oil. Pour over vegetables. Return chicken and any juices to the wok; stir-fry until vegetables are glossy and the sauce has thickened. Serve immediately over rice.

Chicken with Peanut Sauce for One

When you're home alone, this quick dish is very comforting. If someone comes along, it's easily doubled.

SUGGESTED MENU

Chicken with Peanut Sauce for One

Steamed Rice or Noodles

Snow Peas

Wedge of Cantaloupe

1 tbsp	smooth peanut butter	15 mL
2 tsp	soya sauce	10 mL
2 tsp	rice or white wine vinegar	10 mL
Pinch	hot pepper flakes	Pinch
1 tsp	vegetable oil	5 mL
1	skinless boneless chicken breast, cut into (1/2-inch [1 cm]) cubes	1
2 tsp	minced garlic	10 mL
1 tsp	minced ginger root	5 mL

1. In a measuring cup, stir together 1/4 cup (50 mL) water, peanut butter, soya sauce, vinegar and hot pepper flakes.
2. In a nonstick skillet or wok, heat oil over medium-high heat. Add chicken, garlic and ginger; cook, stirring, 2 to 3 minutes or until the chicken is no longer pink inside.
3. Stir in peanut butter mixture; bring to a boil. Reduce heat to low; cook, stirring, for 3 minutes or until thickened.

Sweet-and-Sour Chicken

SERVES 4

Always a family pleaser, this colorful dish is also very pleasing to the eye. Don't let the long ingredient list put you off; it's quick and easy to make.

SHOPPING TIP

Buy boneless breasts, fast-to-cube tenderloins, boneless thighs or chicken already cubed.

SUGGESTED MENU

Sweet-and-Sour Chicken

Rice

Orange Sorbet and Cookies

1/4 cup	packed brown sugar	50 mL
1/4 cup	rice vinegar	50 mL
2 tbsp	soya sauce	25 mL
1 tbsp	Oriental sesame oil	15 mL
1 lb	boneless chicken, cut into cubes	500 g
1	can (14 oz [398 mL]) unsweetened pineapple chunks with juice	1
4 tsp	cornstarch	20 mL
1 tbsp	vegetable oil	15 mL
2	cloves garlic, minced	2
1 tbsp	minced ginger root	15 mL
1	red bell pepper, sliced	1
1 cup	snow peas or sugar snap peas, trimmed	250 mL
1 cup	sliced celery	250 mL
1/4 tsp	hot pepper flakes	1 mL

1. In a medium bowl, stir together the brown sugar, rice vinegar, soya sauce and sesame oil. Add chicken and toss to coat; let stand for 10 minutes while preparing the vegetables.

2. Drain the marinade into a small bowl and whisk in pineapple juice and cornstarch; set aside.

3. In a large wok or skillet, heat the oil over high heat. Add garlic and ginger; stir-fry for 30 seconds or until fragrant. Add chicken; stir-fry for 2 minutes. Add red pepper and stir-fry for 3 minutes.

4. Add peas, celery, pineapple and hot pepper flakes. Stir cornstarch mixture to recombine. Add to the skillet and stir for 2 minutes.

Cajun Wings with Apricot Mustard

Roasting these spicy wings in a hot oven renders them crisp and crusty on the outside and tender and juicy within.

MAKE AHEAD

The wings can be brushed with the spice mixture, covered and refrigerated for up to 8 hours. Bring to room temperature 30 minutes before baking. The sauce can be made up to 1 day ahead, covered and refrigerated.

SUGGESTED MENU

Cajun Wings with
Apricot Mustard

🐦

★ Rice and Peas

🐦

Green Salad

🐦

Sliced Peaches and
Yogurt

★ *Rice and Peas*
Add a small can of kidney
beans, drained, and a
dash of hot pepper sauce
to hot cooked rice. Place
over low heat until the
beans are hot.

PREHEAT OVEN TO 475° F (240° C)
FOIL-LINED BAKING SHEET, GREASED

3 lbs	chicken wings, separated at joints, tips removed	1.5 kg
4	cloves garlic, minced	4
2 tsp	dry mustard	10 mL
2 tsp	paprika	10 mL
1 tsp	ground coriander	5 mL
1 tsp	ground cumin	5 mL
1 tsp	dried thyme	5 mL
1/2 tsp	black pepper	2 mL
1/2 tsp	cayenne pepper	2 mL
1/2 tsp	salt	2 mL
1/3 cup	fresh lime juice or lemon juice	75 mL

APRICOT MUSTARD

1 cup	apricot jam	250 mL
3 tbsp	Dijon mustard	45 mL

1. Reserve tips from wings and set aside for stock if desired.
2. In a small bowl, combine garlic, mustard, paprika, coriander, cumin, thyme, black pepper, cayenne, salt and lime juice. Brush over wings and arrange, meaty-side down, on prepared baking sheet. Bake, uncovered, in preheated oven for 20 to 30 minutes or until brown and crisp, turning once.
3. Apricot Mustard: Meanwhile, in a food processor or blender, purée jam with mustard. Heat in a small saucepan, stirring often, for about 1 minute or until the jam melts. Let cool.

Oriental Fondue

This is one of the world's easiest meals — and a fun one for a family or some close friends. When everything is cooked, the broth turns into a delicious soup. (Make it even heartier by pouring in a lightly beaten egg to cook at the end before adding the soya sauce.) Be sure to keep the raw chicken on a separate plate away from the other food.

MAKE AHEAD

The chicken and vegetables can be prepared ahead, covered well and refrigerated for up to 6 hours. The sauce can also be made ahead, covered and refrigerated for up to 1 day.

SUGGESTED MENU

Oriental Fondue

🐦

Rice

🐦

Orange Wedges

🐦

Fortune Cookies

1 1/2 lbs	skinless boneless chicken breasts	750 g
4	carrots	4
2	small zucchini	2
3 cups	broccoli florets	750 mL
2 cups	mushrooms	500 mL
PEANUT SAUCE		
1/4 cup	peanut butter	50 mL
2 tbsp	chicken stock *or* water	25 mL
2 tbsp	rice vinegar	25 mL
2 tbsp	soya sauce	25 mL
1 tbsp	honey	15 mL
1 tbsp	minced ginger root	15 mL
1 tsp	oriental sesame oil	5 mL
1	clove garlic, minced	1
8 cups	chicken stock	2 L
2 1/2 cups	fine egg noodles	625 mL
1 tbsp	light soya sauce	15 mL
1 tsp	Oriental sesame oil	5 mL
	Salt and pepper	

1. Cut chicken across the grain into very thin slices; place on individual plates. Using a vegetable peeler, cut carrots and zucchini into ribbons by peeling lengthwise. Arrange vegetables on separate individual plates.

2. Peanut Sauce: In a bowl combine peanut butter, stock, vinegar, soya sauce, honey, ginger, sesame oil and garlic; whisk until well blended.

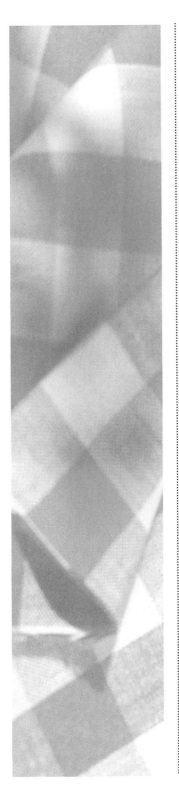

3. In a fondue pot, electric wok or skillet, in the center of the table, bring stock to a boil. Using fondue forks or chopsticks, let each person cook a few pieces of meat and vegetables at a time; cook chicken for 1 to 2 minutes or until no longer pink inside and vegetables are tender-crisp. Serve with Peanut Sauce.

4. When the chicken is eaten, add any remaining vegetables and the noodles to the stock; cook for 4 to 6 minutes or until tender but firm. Stir in soya sauce, sesame oil, and salt and pepper to taste. Serve in heated soup bowls.

Honey-Garlic Chicken Wings

A high oven heat makes the wings crisp and delicious.

MAKE AHEAD

The recipe can be prepared to the end of step 1 up to a day ahead, covered and refrigerated. Bring to room temperature for 30 minutes before baking.

SHOPPING TIPS

Look for wings already separated for quicker preparation.

SUGGESTED MENU

Honey-Garlic Chicken
Wings

Rice

Green Peas

Fruit Salad

PREHEAT OVEN TO 475° F (240° C)
FOIL-LINED BAKING SHEET, GREASED

1/3 cup	hoisin sauce	75 mL
2 tbsp	soya sauce	25 mL
2 tbsp	rice wine	25 mL
2 tbsp	ketchup	25 mL
2 tbsp	liquid honey	25 mL
3	cloves garlic, crushed	3
3 lbs	chicken wings, halved at the joint, tips removed, patted dry	1.5 kg

1. In a large bowl, combine hoisin sauce, soya sauce, wine, ketchup, honey and garlic. Toss wings in sauce mixture to coat well.

2. Arrange the wings meaty-side down on prepared baking sheet. Bake, uncovered, in preheated oven for 15 minutes; turn and bake for 10 minutes longer or until brown, crisp and no longer pink inside.

Cornmeal-Crusted Wings

These easy roasted wings have a nice crunch and zesty flavor.

MAKE AHEAD

Wings can be coated with cornmeal mixture, covered loosely with waxed paper and refrigerated for up to 8 hours. Bring to room temperature for 30 minutes before baking.

SHOPPING TIP

Look for wings already separated for faster preparation. Prepared guacamole is often located in the freezer section or in the produce section of the supermarket.

★ *Citrus Dressing*
Combine 1/3 cup (75 mL) mixed orange and lemon juice with 1 tbsp (15 mL) olive oil, a minced green onion, salt and pepper to taste, a pinch of sugar and a pinch of hot pepper flakes.

PREHEAT OVEN TO 425° F (220° C)
FOIL-LINED BAKING SHEET, GREASED

12	chicken wings, halved at the joint, tips removed	12
1/2 cup	plain yogurt	125 mL
3/4 cup	cornmeal	175 mL
4 tsp	chili powder	20 mL
3/4 tsp	ground cumin	4 mL
3/4 tsp	dried oregano	4 mL
1/2 tsp	granulated sugar	2 mL
1/2 tsp	salt	2 mL
Pinch	cayenne pepper	Pinch

1. In a small bowl, toss the wings with yogurt until well coated. In another bowl, stir together cornmeal, chili powder, cumin, oregano, sugar, salt and cayenne. One by one, add the wings and turn to coat.

2. Arrange wings meaty-side down on prepared baking sheet in a single layer. Bake in preheated oven for about 30 minutes, turning once, until chicken is no longer pink inside.

SUGGESTED MENU

Cornmeal-Crusted Wings

🐦

Guacamole or Bottled Salsa

🐦

Warm Tortillas

🐦

★ Mixed Salad Greens with Sliced Mushrooms and Citrus Dressing

🐦

Chocolate Sundaes

Crisp Curried Chicken Wings with Fresh Coriander Sauce

SERVES 2 OR 3

A cold, refreshing yogurt sauce is a good accompaniment to these crunchy, flavorful wings.

MAKE AHEAD

The wings can be marinated, covered and refrigerated for up to 24 hours. Bring to room temperature for 30 minutes before cooking. The sauce also can be made, covered and refrigerated for up to 24 hours.

SHOPPING TIP

Buy wings already separated to save time. Mango chutney is available in supermarkets, usually in the condiment or international section.

★ *Rice and Green Bean Salad*
Toss cooked rice and steamed sliced green beans with 1/3 cup (75 mL) vegetable oil, 2 tbsp (25 mL) fresh lemon juice, 2 tsp (10 mL) Dijon mustard, and salt and pepper to taste.

PREHEAT OVEN TO 475° F (240° C)
FOIL-LINED BAKING SHEET, GREASED

2 lbs	chicken wings, halved at the joint, tips removed	1 kg
1/4 cup	mango chutney	50 mL
3 tbsp	fresh lime juice or lemon juice	45 mL
2 tbsp	curry powder	25 mL
2 tsp	ground cumin	10 mL
1/2 tsp	salt	2 mL
1/4 tsp	cayenne	1 mL
3/4 cup	plain yogurt	175 mL
1/2 cup	coarsely chopped fresh coriander	125 mL

1. Reserve the wing tips for stock if desired.
2. In a large bowl, stir together chutney, 2 tbsp (25 mL) of the lime juice, curry powder, 1 tsp (5 mL) cumin, salt and half of the cayenne. Add the wings and toss to coat well. Cover and leave at room temperature for 30 minutes.
3. Meanwhile, in a small bowl, stir together yogurt, coriander, remaining lime juice, remaining cumin and remaining cayenne. Cover and refrigerate if making ahead.

4. Arrange the wings, meaty-side down, on prepared baking sheet. Bake in the preheated oven for 15 minutes. Turn wings over and bake for another 10 minutes or until crispy brown and no longer pink inside.

SUGGESTED MENU

Crisp Curried Chicken Wings with Fresh Coriander Sauce

Cold Crisp Cucumber Sticks

★ Rice and Green Bean Salad

Poppadums

Sliced Mangos

QUICK CHICKEN NOODLE SOUP (PAGE 50) ➤

Tex-Mex Wings

Bottled salsa makes a quick and easy glaze for these zesty wings.

PREHEAT OVEN TO 450° F (230° C)
FOIL-LINED BAKING SHEET, GREASED

2 lbs	chicken wings, patted dry, separated at the joints, tips removed	1 kg
1 tbsp	vegetable oil	15 mL
2	jalapeno peppers, minced	2
1 3/4 cups	bottled salsa, preferably chunky	425 mL
1 tbsp	vinegar	15 mL
1 tbsp	Worcestershire sauce	15 mL
1 tsp	chili powder	5 mL
1/2 tsp	paprika	2 mL
1/2 tsp	ground cumin	2 mL
1/2 tsp	dried oregano	2 mL
	Salt and pepper	

1. Arrange wings meaty-side down in a single layer on prepared baking sheet. Bake in preheated oven for 15 minutes, turning once.

2. Meanwhile, in a small saucepan, heat oil over medium-high heat. Add jalapenos and cook for 2 minutes. Stir in salsa, vinegar, Worcestershire sauce, chili powder, paprika, cumin, oregano, and salt and pepper to taste. Bring to a boil; reduce heat and simmer, uncovered, for 5 minutes.

3. Brush jalapeno mixture liberally over browned wings, reserving remaining sauce over low heat. Bake the wings, uncovered, in preheated oven for about 15 to 20 minutes or until tender and glazed, turning once and brushing again with the sauce. Arrange on a heated platter and serve with remaining hot sauce in a bowl.

◄ CHICKEN SALAD NIÇOISE (PAGE 73)

Crunchy Garlic Wings

These crisp wings are delicious by themselves or accompanied by the quick and easy Honey-Mustard Dipping Sauce that follows. This simple recipe is sure to become a family hit.

SHOPPING TIP

Buy wings already separated to save time.

PREHEAT OVEN TO 425° F (220° C)
FOIL-LINED BAKING SHEET, GREASED

1/2 cup	dry bread crumbs	125 mL
1/2 cup	freshly grated Parmesan cheese	125 mL
1/4 cup	chopped fresh parsley	50 mL
1/4 tsp	pepper	1 mL

HONEY-MUSTARD DIPPING SAUCE

1/4 cup	liquid honey	50 mL
4 tsp	Dijon mustard	20 mL
1/4 cup	butter	50 mL
4	cloves garlic, minced	4
3 lbs	chicken wings, halved at the joint, tips removed	1.5 kg

1. In a shallow bowl, mix together bread crumbs, cheese, parsley and pepper. Set aside.
2. Honey-Mustard Sauce: In a small bowl, stir together honey and mustard until smooth and well combined.
3. In a small saucepan over low heat, melt butter with garlic.
4. Dip wings in the butter mixture, then in the bread crumb mixture and coat well. Arrange meaty-side down in a single layer on prepared baking sheet. Bake in pre-heated oven for 25 minutes or until chicken is no longer pink inside, turning once. Serve hot with Honey-Mustard Dipping Sauce if desired.

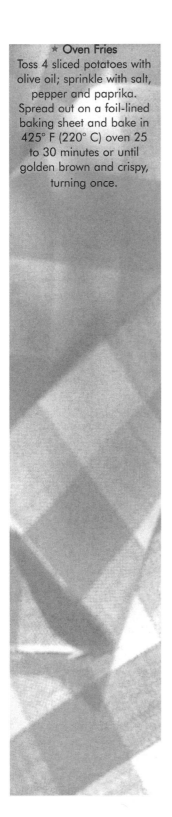

★ **Oven Fries**
Toss 4 sliced potatoes with
olive oil; sprinkle with salt,
pepper and paprika.
Spread out on a foil-lined
baking sheet and bake in
425° F (220° C) oven 25
to 30 minutes or until
golden brown and crispy,
turning once.

SUGGESTED MENU

Crunchy Garlic Wings
with Honey-Mustard
Dipping Sauce

❧

★ Oven Fries

❧

Green Peas

❧

Applesauce and
Cookies

Kids' Wings

I developed this crunchy wing recipe for kids' lunch boxes in a *Canadian Living* article, but it is a good quick supper item to make for the kids when you are going out; however, feel free to double the recipe, since you'll find yourself (and any other adults) nibbling on them too.

MAKE AHEAD

Wings can be coated, covered and refrigerated for up to 4 hours before baking. Bring to room temperature for 30 minutes before cooking.

SHOPPING TIP

Look for separated wings in the supermarket to save time. If buttermilk is not in your refrigerator, combine 1/4 cup (50 mL) sweet milk with 1 tsp (5 mL) vinegar; let stand for 15 minutes.

★ Instant Macaroni and Cheese

Cook 1 1/2 cups (375 mL) macaroni, drain and combine it with 1 cup (250 mL) shredded Cheddar cheese, 1/4 cup (50 mL) yogurt, 1 tbsp (15 mL) butter, 1 tbsp (15mL) Dijon mustard, and salt and pepper to taste.

PREHEAT OVEN TO 425° F (220° C)
FOIL-LINED BAKING SHEET, GREASED

1 lb	chicken wings, separated at the joint, tips removed	500 g
1/2 cup	all-purpose flour	125 mL
1 tbsp	wheat germ	15 mL
1 1/2 tsp	paprika	7 mL
1/2 tsp	dried marjoram	2 mL
1/2 tsp	dry mustard	2 mL
1/2 tsp	salt	2 mL
1/4 tsp	pepper	1 mL
1/4 cup	buttermilk	50 mL

1. Reserve tips of wings for stock or soup.
2. In a plastic bag, shake together flour, wheat germ, paprika, marjoram, mustard, salt and pepper. Pour the buttermilk into a shallow dish.
3. In batches, shake the wings in the flour mixture, shaking off the excess back into the bag. Dip into buttermilk; shake again in the flour mixture. Arrange on prepared baking sheet. Bake in preheated oven for about 30 minutes until golden brown and the chicken is no longer pink inside.

SUGGESTED MENU

Kids' Wings

🐦

Carrot and Celery Sticks

🐦

Coleslaw

🐦

Potato Salad or
★ Instant Macaroni and Cheese

🐦

Ice Cream Sundaes

Chicken and Bean Burritos

A fun supper for kids, these burritos are quick and easy to make with inexpensive ground chicken.

MAKE AHEAD

Chicken and bean filling can be made up to 1 day ahead, covered and refrigerated; reheat in skillet over low heat. The mixture can also be frozen for up to 2 months. Thaw in the refrigerator and reheat.

SUGGESTED MENU

Chicken and Bean
Burritos

🌿

Green Salad

🌿

Chocolate Sundaes

1 tbsp	vegetable oil	15 mL
1 lb	ground chicken	500 g
1	small red bell pepper, chopped	1
2	green onions, sliced	2
2 tsp	ground cumin	10 mL
1/2 tsp	dried oregano	2 mL
1/4 tsp	hot pepper flakes, or to taste	1 mL
1	can (19 oz [540 mL]) black beans or kidney beans, drained and rinsed	1
1 cup	bottled salsa	250 mL
2 tbsp	chopped fresh coriander	25 mL
	Salt	
6	flour tortillas (10-inch [25 cm])	6
	Additional salsa, sour cream and sliced green onions	

1. In a large heavy skillet, heat oil over medium-high heat. Add chicken, pepper and onions; cook for 7 minutes, stirring often and breaking up the chicken.

2. Stir in cumin, oregano and hot pepper flakes. Add beans, salsa and coriander; simmer until most of the liquid is evaporated, mashing some of the beans against the side of the skillet. Add salt to taste or, if desired, more hot pepper flakes.

3. Meanwhile, steam the tortillas by setting them on a rack over 1/2 inch (1 cm) simmering water in a covered skillet for 30 seconds.

4. Set 1 tortilla on the counter and mound one-sixth of the chicken mixture on lower half, leaving a 1/2-inch (1 cm) border along edges. Roll up filling tightly in tortilla, folding in sides to enclose filling. Fill and roll remaining tortillas. Spoon additional salsa, sour cream and green onions on top.

Roasted Chicken Fajitas

Roasting the chicken strips and vegetables in the oven not only gives extra flavor to the fajitas, but it is a fast and easy way of making them.

VARIATION

Sautéed Chicken Fajitas
Instead of roasting the chicken and vegetables, sauté the chicken strips in half the oil over medium-high heat for 3 to 5 minutes or until browned. Remove from the pan; add remaining oil and vegetables; cook for 5 minutes, stirring often.

SHOPPING TIP

Buy chicken strips that are already cut and packaged for stir-fries.

SUGGESTED MENU

Roasted Chicken Fajitas

Green Salad

Ice Cream

PREHEAT OVEN TO 400° F (200° C)
LARGE SHALLOW ROASTING PAN, GREASED

1 lb	skinless boneless chicken breasts	500 g
2 tbsp	vegetable oil	25 mL
1 tbsp	fresh lime juice	15 mL
1 tsp	chili powder	5 mL
1/2 tsp	ground cumin	2 mL
2	large onions, in wedges	2
2	large red bell peppers, cut into wide strips	2
	Salt and pepper	
8	large flour tortillas	8
1 cup	shredded lettuce (optional)	250 mL
2	avocados, peeled and sliced	2
	Tomato salsa	
	Sour cream	

1. Cut chicken crosswise into 5 or 6 strips. Toss with half the oil; add lime juice, chili powder and cumin; set aside.

2. Combine onions and peppers in prepared roasting pan. Drizzle with remaining oil; sprinkle with salt and pepper. Add chicken mixture; stir to combine and spread out in the pan. Roast in preheated oven, stirring once or twice, for 20 to 25 minutes or until chicken is no longer pink inside and vegetables are tender.

3. Meanwhile, wrap tortillas tightly in foil and place in the oven for 10 minutes to heat.

4. Transfer chicken and vegetables to a heated platter and serve with tortillas, lettuce, avocados, salsa and sour cream. Have each diner spoon some chicken mixture into a tortilla, top with lettuce (if desired), avocado, salsa and sour cream to taste; roll up to eat.

Chinese Chicken Roll-Ups

Rolling up this Oriental ground chicken mixture in lettuce leaves is messy, but fun. If you wish, serve it in lettuce cups with a knife and fork; or you can even mix cultures and roll it up in warm tortillas. Although the recipe looks long, it's easy and all you need for supper.

SHOPPING TIPS

These days, you can find oyster sauce, sesame oil and hoisin sauce in most supermarkets. You will probably have to locate Chinese dried mushrooms in an Oriental grocery store, but they keep indefinitely in a sealed container; so buy a good quantity. Seek out low-salt soya sauce, usually also available in supermarkets.

SUGGESTED MENU
Chinese Chicken
Roll-Ups

Melon Wedges

6	dried Chinese black mushrooms *or* cloud ear mushrooms	6
2 tbsp	oyster sauce	25 mL
2 tbsp	soya sauce	25 mL
2 tbsp	dry sherry *or* rice wine	25 mL
1 tsp	granulated sugar	5 mL
1 tsp	cornstarch	5 mL
2 tbsp	vegetable oil	25 mL
1 lb	lean ground chicken	500 g
2	green onions, chopped	2
1 tbsp	minced ginger root	15 mL
4	cloves garlic, thinly sliced	4
3/4 cup	minced water chestnuts	175 mL
1 tsp	oriental sesame oil	5 mL
	Salt and pepper	
	Leaf lettuce leaves	
	Hoisin sauce	

1. Soak mushrooms in hot water for 20 minutes; drain, remove any hard stems and thinly slice.

2. In a small bowl, stir together oyster sauce, soya sauce, sherry, sugar and cornstarch until dissolved; set aside.

3. In a wok, heat oil over high heat. Add chicken, green onions, ginger and garlic; stir-fry for 2 minutes.

4. Add chestnuts and reserved mushrooms; stir-fry for 2 minutes. Boil to reduce the liquid to 2 tbsp (25 mL). Stir in sesame oil and oyster sauce mixture; stir-fry for 1 or 2 minutes or until slightly thickened. Season with salt and pepper. Transfer to a large warm platter; surround with lettuce leaves and serve hoisin sauce in a bowl. Have each person brush about 1/2 tsp (2 mL) hoisin on each lettuce leaf, then spoon some of the chicken mixture into the center and roll up to enclose.

Substantial Soups

Chicken Soup with Lentils and Lemon

If you like lemon, you'll love this low-fat version of a Lebanese favorite.

Homemade chicken broth lets you control the sodium, but 2 cans (each 10 oz [284 mL]) of broth and 2 cans of water make up 5 cups (1.25 L) when you don't have homemade on hand.

SUGGESTED MENU

Chicken Soup with Lentils and Lemon

Grain Bread

Fresh Fruit Salad

5 cups	chicken broth	1.25 L
2	bone-in chicken breasts	2
3	carrots, sliced	3
2	celery stalks, sliced	2
1	onion, chopped	1
2	cloves garlic, minced	2
1 tsp	grated lemon zest	5 mL
1	bay leaf	1
	Salt and pepper	
1	can (19 oz [540 mL]) lentils, rinsed and drained	1
1/2 cup	chopped fresh parsley	125 mL
1/4 cup	fresh lemon juice	50 mL
1 tsp	ground cumin	5 mL
3/4 cup	hot cooked rice	175 mL

1. In a large saucepan, bring broth to a simmer. Add chicken, carrots, celery, onion, garlic, lemon zest, bay leaf and 1/2 tsp (2 mL) salt. Bring back to a simmer, cover and cook for 20 minutes or until the chicken is no longer pink inside. Remove chicken. Add lentils and cook for 5 minutes.

2. Meanwhile, remove and discard chicken skin and bones; dice the chicken and return to the soup with parsley, lemon juice and cumin. Add salt and pepper to taste. Discard bay leaf.

3. Place a large spoonful of rice in each soup bowl and pour the soup over top.

Middle Eastern Chicken Soup

A little leftover chicken and canned broth make a quick and wholesome main course soup. Serve with a dollop of non-fat yogurt or a splash of fresh lemon juice if you wish.

VARIATION

Chunky Vegetable Chicken Soup

Omit the chickpeas and spinach. Substitute 1/2 tsp (2 mL) dried thyme for the cumin. Add another carrot and 1 coarsely chopped potato. Add 1 red bell pepper and 1 zucchini, coarsely chopped, halfway through the cooking time.

MAKE AHEAD

The soup can be covered and refrigerated for up to 1 day ahead.

SUGGESTED MENU

Middle Eastern Chicken Soup

🐦

Tuna Salad Filled Pitas

🐦

Fresh Fruit

1	can (10 oz [284 mL]) chicken broth	1
1	can (19 oz [540 mL]) chickpeas, rinsed and drained	1
1 cup	chopped or shredded cooked chicken	250 mL
1	small onion, chopped	1
1	carrot, chopped	1
1	clove garlic, chopped	1
1 tsp	dried oregano	5 mL
1 tsp	ground cumin	5 mL
Half	pkg (10 oz [284 g]) fresh spinach, stemmed and coarsely chopped	Half
	Salt and pepper	

1. In a medium saucepan, combine the broth, 1 1/2 cans water, chickpeas, chicken, onion, carrot, garlic, oregano and cumin. Bring to a boil, reduce heat and simmer, covered, for 15 minutes.

2. Stir in the spinach and cook, uncovered, for 2 minutes. Season to taste with salt and pepper.

Quick Chunky Minestrone

Canned chickpeas or beans add lots of texture and nutrients to this "whole meal" soup that makes good use of some of Sunday's leftover roast chicken. Don't let the rather long ingredient list put you off; the soup is quick and easy to make.

MAKE AHEAD

The soup can be made and refrigerated in an airtight container up to 2 days ahead or frozen for up to 3 months.

SUGGESTED MENU

Quick Chunky
Minestrone

★ Garlic Flatbread

Crisp Green Salad

Melon Slices

★ Garlic Flatbread
Combine olive oil with crushed garlic and Italian herb seasoning. Brush the mixture over store-bought flatbread and bake in a hot oven until golden brown.

4	slices bacon, diced	4
2	celery stalks, sliced	2
1	onion, chopped	1
1	carrot, sliced	1
1	clove garlic, minced	1
1	can (19 oz [540 mL]) tomatoes	1
4 cups	chicken stock	1 L
1/4 tsp	crumbled dried sage	1 mL
1/4 tsp	thyme	1 mL
1	can (19 oz [540 mL]) chickpeas *or* white kidney or Romano beans, rinsed and drained	1
4 oz	cut fresh or frozen green beans	125 g
1 cup	chopped or shredded cooked chicken	250 mL
1/4 cup	macaroni or any small pasta	50 mL
	Salt and pepper	
1/4 cup	freshly grated Parmesan cheese	50 mL

1   In a large saucepan, cook bacon over medium heat until crisp; remove with a slotted spoon and set aside to drain on paper towels.

2. Pour off all but 1 tbsp (15 mL) drippings from the pan. Add celery, onion, carrot and garlic; cook, stirring occasionally, for 5 minutes. Add tomatoes, breaking up with the back of a spoon. Add chicken stock, sage and thyme; bring to a boil. Reduce heat, cover and simmer for 5 minutes.

3. Add chickpeas, beans, chicken and macaroni; cook for 8 to 10 minutes or until the macaroni is tender but firm. Return cooked bacon to the pan. Season with salt and pepper to taste. Top each serving with Parmesan cheese.

Chicken and Pasta Soup with Almonds

SERVES 3 OR 4

This intriguing chicken soup is full of interesting flavors and makes a nice light main course.

SHOPPING TIP

If you don't have homemade chicken broth, 2 cans (each 10 oz [284 mL]) broth and 2 cans of water make 5 cups (1.25 L).

SUGGESTED MENU

Chicken and Pasta Soup with Almonds

★ Grilled Prosciutto and Fontina Sandwiches

Ice Cream Sundaes

★ *Grilled Prosciutto and Fontina Sandwiches*
Place thin slices of prosciutto, Fontina cheese and fresh basil leaves between thick slices of Italian bread. Brush with olive oil and grill in a heavy skillet over medium heat, turning once, until golden brown on the outside and the cheese melts.

5 cups	chicken broth	1.25 L
1/2 cup	small dry pasta	125 mL
3 tbsp	olive oil	45 mL
1/2 cup	sliced almonds	125 mL
2	cloves garlic, minced	2
2	green onions, coarsely chopped	2
1/2 cup	packed parsley sprigs	125 mL
1/4 cup	freshly grated Parmesan cheese	50 mL
1 tbsp	fresh lemon juice	15 mL
1 lb	skinless boneless chicken breasts or thighs, cut into (3/4-inch [2 cm]) cubes	500 g
	Salt and pepper	

1. In a large saucepan, bring the broth to a boil. Add pasta and cook 5 to 8 minutes or until tender but firm.

2. Meanwhile, in a large skillet, heat 2 tbsp (25 mL) of the oil over medium-low heat. Add almonds and sauté for 2 minutes. Add garlic and cook for 1 minute. Set aside half of almond-garlic mixture for garnish; transfer the remainder to a food processor. Add onions, parsley, cheese and lemon juice. Purée until smooth.

3. Add remaining oil to skillet; heat over medium-high heat. Sprinkle chicken with salt and pepper. Add to skillet and sauté for 4 to 5 minutes or until golden and no longer pink inside.

4. Add chicken and puréed mixture to soup. Adjust seasoning to taste. Garnish with remaining almond-garlic mixture.

Chicken Tortellini Soup with Peas

Convenient ingredients like tortellini, frozen vegetables and cans of chicken broth turn Sunday's leftover chicken into a hearty meal in no time.

SUGGESTED MENU

Chicken Tortellini Soup with Peas

❧

★ Tomato Bruschetta

❧

Ice Cream Sundaes

★ *Tomato Bruschetta*
Top thick slices of toasted Italian bread with fresh tomato slices; sprinkle with chopped basil, salt and pepper; drizzle with olive oil.

3	cloves garlic, minced	3
8 oz	fresh or frozen cheese tortellini	250 g
2	cans (10 oz [284 mL]) chicken broth	2
1 cup	frozen peas	250 mL
1 cup	diced cooked chicken	250 mL
1/4 tsp	pepper	1 mL
2 tbsp	chopped green onions	25 mL
1/4 cup	freshly grated Parmesan cheese	50 mL

1. In a large pot, bring 3 cups (750 mL) water and the garlic to a boil. Add the tortellini; return to a boil. Reduce heat to medium-high; cook, stirring occasionally, for 10 minutes if fresh or 15 minutes if frozen, or according to the package instructions.

2. Add chicken broth and peas; return to a boil and cook for 2 minutes. Add chicken; cook for 1 minute. Stir in pepper and green onions. Serve sprinkled with Parmesan cheese.

Thick Rice Soup with Chicken

A bit like congee (the satisfying Chinese rice soup that might be breakfast fare), this comforting soup has a more complex flavor, but is still filling and warming — just the answer when you're hungry and cold, and think there's nothing in the house for supper.

SHOPPING TIP

Homemade broth or stock is always best, but for convenience, 2 cans (each 10 oz [284 mL]) broth and 2 cans of water make 5 cups (1.25 L) of chicken broth.

2 tbsp	vegetable oil	25 mL
1 tbsp	minced ginger root	15 mL
2	cloves garlic, minced	2
1	small onion, minced	1
1 lb	skinless boneless chicken, diced	500 g
1 cup	white rice (regular or parboiled)	250 mL
5 cups	chicken broth	1.25 L
2 tbsp	dry sherry	25 mL
1 tbsp	soya sauce	15 mL
1 tsp	sesame oil	5 mL
1/4 tsp	hot pepper flakes	1 mL
	Salt and pepper	
2	green onions, sliced	2
1/4 cup	chopped peanuts	50 mL

1. In a large saucepan, heat oil over medium–high heat. Add ginger, garlic and onion; cook for 1 minute. Add chicken; cook, stirring, for 3 to 5 minutes or until no longer pink inside.

2. Stir in rice, broth, sherry, soya sauce, sesame oil and hot pepper flakes. Bring to a boil; reduce heat and simmer for 20 minutes or until the chicken and rice are cooked through. Stir in salt and pepper to taste.

3. Garnish each serving with green onions and peanuts.

SUGGESTED MENU

Thick Rice Soup with Chicken

Spinach Salad with Bean Sprouts and Orange Slices

Melon Wedges

Hot and Sour Soup

The Cantonese think of soup not only as a delicious food but also as essential therapy for rehydrating the body and skin. I think you'll agree that this comforting soup goes a long way, too, as therapy for the soul on a cold night. You could make a meal of this hearty soup, but it will serve more than 4 if you make it part of a multi-dish Chinese meal.

MAKE AHEAD

Soup can be prepared ahead to the end of step 2. Reheat before proceeding with recipe.

1 cup	Chinese dried mushrooms	250 mL
8 cups	chicken broth	2 L
1 lb	skinless boneless chicken, slivered	500 g
1 1/2 cups	matchstick-cut bamboo shoots (fresh or canned, rinsed)	375 mL
12 oz	extra-firm tofu, cut into thin julienne strips	375 g
2 tbsp	rice vinegar	25 mL
1 tbsp	Worcestershire sauce or Chinese black vinegar	15 mL
1 tbsp	rice wine or sherry	15 mL
1 tbsp	minced ginger root	15 mL
1/2 tsp	salt	2 mL
1/2 tsp	pepper	2 mL
2 tbsp	cornstarch	25 mL
1 cup	frozen peas	250 mL
1	egg, lightly beaten	1
2 tsp	sesame oil	10 mL
1 tsp	chili oil, or to taste	5 mL
1	green onion, finely chopped	1

1. In a small bowl, cover mushrooms with 3/4 cup (175 mL) warm water and let soak while preparing the remaining ingredients, preferably for 30 minutes. Drain, discarding water. Trim off any tough stems; slice the caps into thin julienne strips.

2. In a large pot, bring chicken broth to a boil. Add mushrooms, chicken and bamboo shoots; return to a boil. Reduce heat to medium, cover and simmer for 3 minutes. Add tofu, vinegar, Worcestershire sauce, rice wine, ginger, salt and pepper. Bring to a boil. Reduce heat and adjust seasoning to taste.

3. Dissolve cornstarch in 1/4 cup (50 mL) cold water. Slowly add to the hot soup, stirring constantly; simmer until thickened. Stir in peas and cook for another 1 to 2 minutes.

SUGGESTED MENU

Hot and Sour Soup

❧

Szechuan Chicken and
Peanuts with Chili
Peppers (page 19)

❧

White Rice

❧

Stir-Fried Assorted
Vegetables

❧

Orange Wedges

4. Remove pot from heat and slowly add the beaten egg, pouring in a thin stream around the edge and carefully stirring once or twice so that the cooked egg forms streamers.

5. Transfer to a heated tureen or serving bowl. Carefully stir in sesame oil and chili oil. Sprinkle with green onion and serve immediately.

Quick Chicken Noodle Soup

This soothing and satisfying soup is made in minutes with chicken left from Sunday's roast.

SUGGESTED MENU

Quick Chicken Noodle Soup

Wholegrain Bread or Rolls

Fresh Spinach Salad

Applesauce and Cookies

2 tbsp	butter	25 mL
1 cup	diced carrots	250 mL
4	green onions, sliced	4
5 cups	chicken broth	1.25 L
1	bay leaf	1
	Salt and pepper	
4 oz	very thin egg noodles	125 g
1 cup	diced cooked chicken	250 mL
1/2 cup	frozen peas	125 mL

1. In a large saucepan, melt the butter over medium heat. Add carrots and cook for 3 minutes. Stir in green onions. Gradually stir in broth. Add bay leaf and salt and pepper to taste. Bring to a boil; reduce heat, cover and simmer for 3 to 5 minutes or until the carrots are almost tender.

2. Return soup to a boil. Add noodles, chicken and peas; simmer, uncovered, for 3 to 5 minutes until chicken is heated through and noodles are tender.

3. Remove bay leaf and season to taste.

Mediterranean Chicken Soup

This hearty soup with quick-cooking vegetables and couscous is loaded with flavor, but takes only minutes to make.

SHOPPING TIPS

For convenience, look for chicken already cut into strips. If you don't have homemade broth, 2 cans (10 oz [284 mL]) of chicken broth and 2 cans of water will make 5 cups (1.25 L).

SUGGESTED MENU

Mediterranean Chicken Soup

Warm Pita Breads

Green Salad

Fresh Fruit

1 lb	skinless boneless chicken breasts or thighs, cut into thin strips	500 g
1	red bell pepper, chopped	1
1	yellow bell pepper, chopped	1
5 cups	chicken broth	1.25 L
1 tsp	ground cumin	5 mL
1/4 tsp	hot pepper flakes	1 mL
1/4 tsp	dried oregano	1 mL
2	small zucchini, halved lengthwise and sliced	2
1/2 cup	chopped red onions	125 mL
1/4 cup	chopped fresh coriander *or* parsley	50 mL
	Salt and pepper	
1/2 cup	couscous	125 mL

1. In a large saucepan over medium heat, combine chicken with peppers, broth, cumin, hot pepper flakes and oregano. Heat just until simmering.
2. Add zucchini and onions. Bring back to a simmer. Cover and cook for 10 minutes or until chicken is cooked through. Stir in the coriander; season to taste with salt and pepper.
3. Meanwhile, in a bowl combine couscous with 1 cup (250 mL) boiling water; let sit for 5 minutes.
4. To serve, divide couscous among 4 warm soup bowls and ladle soup on top.

Chicken Cheese Chowder

A bit of cooked chicken from your weekend roast teams up with cheese for extra protein in this quick and hearty main-course soup. For a fun garnish, use popcorn.

The soup is also tasty without the additional fat of cheese.

SHOPPING TIP

If you don't have homemade broth on hand, 1 can (10 oz [284 mL]) chicken broth and 1 can water will give you the quantity needed.

2 tbsp	butter	25 mL
1	large potato, diced	1
1	onion, chopped	1
1/4 cup	all-purpose flour	50 mL
2 1/2 cups	chicken broth	625 mL
1 1/4 cups	milk	300 mL
1/2 tsp	Worcestershire sauce	2 mL
1/2 tsp	dried marjoram	2 mL
1 cup	diced cooked chicken	250 mL
1 cup	frozen corn kernels, thawed	250 mL
1/4 cup	chopped fresh parsley	50 mL
	Salt and pepper	
1 cup	diced Cheddar cheese	250 mL

1. In a large saucepan, melt butter over medium heat. Add potato and onion; cook, stirring often, for 10 minutes. Blend in the flour; cook for 1 minute, stirring constantly. Add the broth, milk, Worcestershire sauce and marjoram. Stir until slightly thick and bubbly.

2. Stir in the chicken and corn to heat through. Add parsley and salt and pepper to taste. Divide cheese among 4 warm soup bowls and ladle soup on top.

SUGGESTED MENU

Chicken Cheese Chowder

Whole grain Rolls

Celery, Carrot and Cucumber Sticks

Chocolate Sundaes

Chicken and Black Bean Soup

SERVES 4 TO 6

You'll want to keep your cupboard stocked with cans of the vegetables called for in this zesty soup that's sure to become a favorite way to use some of Sunday's roast chicken.

MAKE AHEAD

The soup can be made up to 2 days ahead, covered and refrigerated. Reheat gently, stirring often, before serving.

SHOPPING TIP

Two cans (each 10 oz [284 mL]) chicken broth and 2 cans water make 5 cups (1.25 L) of broth if you do not have any homemade on hand.

SUGGESTED MENU

Chicken and Black Bean Soup

Warm Corn or Flour Tortillas

Orange Wedges

5 cups	chicken broth	1.25 L
2	cans (19 oz [540 mL]) black beans, rinsed and drained	2
1	can (14 oz [398 mL]) tomatoes, preferably stewed	1
1	can (12 oz [341 mL]) corn kernels, drained *or* 1 1/2 cups (375 mL) frozen corn	1
3	cloves garlic, minced	3
2	jalapeno peppers, minced	2
2 tsp	ground cumin	10 mL
2 tsp	dried oregano	10 mL
1 1/2 cups	cubed cooked chicken	375 mL
1/4 cup	fresh lime juice	50 mL
	Salt and pepper	
	Sour cream	
	Chopped fresh coriander	

1. In a large saucepan, combine broth, beans, tomatoes, corn, garlic, jalapeno peppers, cumin and oregano. Bring to a boil; reduce heat and simmer, uncovered, for 10 minutes. Mash some of the beans against the side of the pan to help thicken the soup.

2. Add chicken, lime juice and salt and pepper to taste; simmer for 1 to 2 minutes until chicken is heated through. Serve in warm bowls, each garnished with a dollop of sour cream and a sprinkling of coriander.

Satisfying Salads

Mustard-Grilled Chicken Salad

The grilled chicken stays moist and flavorful beneath its mustardy coating for this warm "whole meal" salad.

MAKE AHEAD

The greens can be washed and dried and the dressing can be made and refrigerated up to one day ahead. The chicken can be marinated, covered, in the refrigerator up to 4 hours ahead. Warm to room temperature for 30 minutes before grilling.

DRESSING

1/3 cup	olive oil	75 mL
2 tbsp	white wine vinegar	25 mL
2 tsp	Dijon mustard	10 mL
1	clove garlic, minced	1
	Salt and pepper	
2 tbsp	olive oil	25 mL
2 tbsp	Dijon mustard	25 mL
1 tbsp	white wine vinegar	15 mL
1	clove garlic, minced	1
1 tsp	dried marjoram	5 mL
1 tsp	paprika	5 mL
1/4 tsp	cayenne	1 mL
4	skinless boneless chicken breasts (1 1/2 lbs [750 g] total)	4
8 cups	washed and torn mixed salad greens	2 L
2	tomatoes, diced	2

1. Dressing: In a bowl, whisk together the oil, vinegar, mustard, garlic and salt and pepper to taste. Set aside.

2. In a non-metallic dish just large enough to hold the chicken in a single layer, combine oil, mustard, vinegar, garlic, marjoram, paprika and cayenne. Add chicken, turning to coat on both sides. Marinate, covered, for 30 minutes at room temperature.

3. Remove chicken from marinade; place on a greased barbecue grill and cook over medium-high heat for 10 to 12 minutes, turning every 4 minutes or until the juices run clear when the chicken is pierced with a skewer and is no longer pink inside. Transfer to a cutting board; cover with foil. Discard any remaining marinade.

4. In a large bowl, toss the greens with just enough dressing to coat the leaves lightly. Divide among 4 plates.

5. Cut chicken crosswise into slices; arrange on top of the greens. Garnish with tomatoes; sprinkle with remaining dressing.

Chicken and Cantaloupe Salad with Toasted Pecans

Everyone loves chicken salad. This colorful and elegant version is just right for a party.

MAKE AHEAD

The chicken can be poached a day ahead. Leave in liquid, cover and refrigerate; or cool in liquid, prepare as for salad, wrap and refrigerate. Salad can be made to the end of step 3, covered and refrigerated for several hours.

PREPARATION HINT

To toast pecans, spread out on a cookie sheet and set in a 350° F (180° C) oven for about 5 minutes or until fragrant.

SUGGESTED MENU

Chicken and Cantaloupe Salad with Toasted Pecans

Warm Croissants

Assorted Cookies and Squares

DRESSING

1 cup	mayonnaise	250 mL
2 tbsp	cider vinegar	25 mL
2 tbsp	liquid honey	25 mL
1 tsp	curry powder	5 mL
1/2 tsp	ground ginger	2 mL
	Salt	
12	bone-in chicken breasts	12
1/2 cup	cider vinegar	125 mL
1 tsp	salt	5 mL
2 cups	thinly sliced celery	500 mL
1/2 cup	thinly sliced red onions	125 mL
2	small cantaloupes	2
1 cup	toasted pecan halves	250 mL
	Boston or romaine lettuce leaves	

1. Dressing: In a bowl whisk together mayonnaise, vinegar, honey, curry powder, ginger, and salt to taste. Refrigerate.

2. In a large stainless steel saucepan, combine chicken, vinegar and salt; cover with cold water. Gradually bring to a boil; reduce heat to low and simmer, covered, for 20 minutes or until the chicken is no longer pink inside. Let cool slightly in poaching liquid.

3. Remove chicken from the liquid, discarding liquid. Remove and discard the skin and bones. Cut or shred meat into bite-sized pieces and place in a large bowl. Add celery and onion. Pour on dressing and toss lightly to mix. Cover and refrigerate if making ahead.

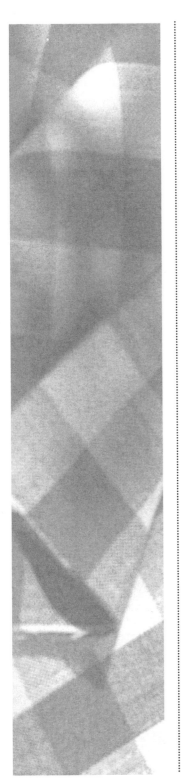

4. Peel and seed cantaloupes. Cut one into thin wedges and reserve for garnish. Using melon baller, make tiny balls from the second (or cut into cubes); stir into salad with 3/4 cup (175 mL) of the pecans.

5. Line a large serving platter or individual plates with lettuce leaves. Mound salad in the center; surround with cantaloupe wedges and sprinkle with remaining pecans.

Chunky Barbecue Chicken Salad

You won't believe how good this simple salad is. Leftover barbecued chicken is best; or use a store-bought rotisserie chicken you can pick up on your way home from work.

SUGGESTED MENU

Chunky Barbecue
Chicken Salad

★ Hot Garlic Bread

Corn on the Cob

Sliced Tomatoes

Blueberries and
Cream

★ Hot Garlic Bread
Blend minced garlic with soft butter and spread liberally onto cut side of lengthwise sliced baguette; wrap in foil and heat in the oven.

4 cups	cooked chicken, cut into 1 1/2-inch (3 cm) cubes	1 L
1	red bell pepper, coarsely diced	1
1/3 cup	diced onions	75 mL
1/3 cup	bottled barbecue sauce	75 mL
1/3 cup	mayonnaise	75 mL
	Salt and pepper	
	Lettuce cups	

1. In a large bowl, combine chicken, red pepper and onions.
2. In another bowl, stir together barbecue sauce and mayonnaise. Season to taste with salt and pepper. Pour dressing over chicken mixture and toss to coat. Serve in lettuce cups.

Chicken Waldorf Salad

An old favorite quickly becomes a main course with some of Sunday's roast chicken.

2 cups	cooked chicken, cut into 1/2-inch (1 cm) cubes	500 mL
3/4 cup	toasted walnut pieces	175 mL
1/2 cup	seedless raisins	125 mL
2	stalks celery, sliced	2
1	large red apple, diced	1
2/3 cup	light mayonnaise	150 mL
2 tbsp	fresh lemon juice	25 mL
2 tsp	Dijon mustard	10 mL
	Salt and pepper	
	Lettuce cups	

1. In a large bowl, stir together chicken, walnuts, raisins, celery and apple.
2. In a small bowl, stir together mayonnaise, lemon juice, mustard, and salt and pepper to taste. Add to chicken mixture and stir to coat well. Serve in lettuce cups.

SUGGESTED MENU

Chicken Waldorf Salad

Crusty Brown Rolls

Carrot Sticks

Sugared Blueberries and Yogurt

Chicken Salad with Feta Cheese and Spinach

HERB DRESSING

2	cloves garlic, minced	2
1 tbsp	minced fresh oregano (or 1/2 tsp [2 mL] dried)	15 mL
1 tbsp	minced fresh mint (or 1/2 tsp [2 mL] dried)	15 mL
1 tsp	granulated sugar	5 mL
Pinch	cinnamon	Pinch
2 tbsp	fresh lemon juice	25 mL
2 tbsp	red wine vinegar	25 mL
1/3 cup	olive oil	75 mL
2 1/2 cups	cooked chicken, cut into 1/2-inch (1 cm) cubes	625 mL
1	small cucumber, halved lengthwise and thinly sliced	1
12	cherry tomatoes, halved	12
8	large black olives, pitted and halved	8
4 oz	feta cheese, cubed	125 g
	Salt and pepper	
Half	pkg (10 oz [284 g]) fresh spinach trimmed, washed and dried	Half

1. Herb Dressing: In a small bowl, combine garlic, oregano, mint, sugar, cinnamon, lemon juice and vinegar. Gradually whisk in oil.

2. In a large bowl, combine chicken, cucumber, tomatoes, olives and feta. Add the dressing and toss to coat; add salt and pepper to taste. Arrange spinach on dinner plates and spoon salad on top.

Chicken Salad with Corn and Hearts Of Palm

I gained a great fondness for hearts of palm at a cooking school in Costa Rica. They have a lovely refreshing taste that's perfect in this flavorful salad.

MAKE AHEAD

Salad can be made, covered and refrigerated (without the lettuce) for up to 1 day ahead. Bring to room temperature before serving.

SHOPPING TIP

Look for hearts of palm in cans or jars in the specialty or international sections of your supermarket.

★ *Bananas Flambéed with Rum*
Add halved (lengthwise) bananas to melted butter in a skillet and cook over medium-low heat for 1 minute. Turn, sprinkle with brown sugar and cook another minute. Pour rum over top and ignite; shake until the flame goes out and serve with the sauce over top.

LIME DRESSING

1 tsp	finely grated lime zest	5 mL
2 tbsp	fresh lime juice	25 mL
1 tsp	chili powder	5 mL
1/3 cup	olive oil	75 mL
	Salt and pepper	
3 cups	cubed or shredded cooked chicken	750 mL
2 cups	cooked corn kernels	500 mL
1 cup	thinly sliced (1/4-inch [5 mm]) hearts of palm	250 mL
1/4 cup	diced red bell pepper	50 mL
1/4 cup	diced onion	50 mL
	Lettuce leaves	

1. Lime Dressing: In a small bowl, stir together lime zest, juice and chili powder. Gradually whisk in the oil. Season to taste with salt and pepper.
2. In a large bowl, combine chicken, corn, hearts of palm, pepper and onion. Pour dressing over top. Transfer to lettuce-lined bowl or platter to serve.

SUGGESTED MENU

Chilled Tomato Soup

🐓

Chicken Salad with Corn and Hearts of Palm

🐓

Warm Tortillas

🐓

★ Bananas Flambéed with Rum

Skillet Chicken Salad

SERVES 4

This hot colorful salad is just the answer for a light supper.

4	skinless boneless chicken breasts	4
1	red bell pepper	1
Half	bunch broccoli	Half
1/4 cup	vegetable oil	50 mL
1/4 cup	chicken stock	50 mL
3 tbsp	white wine vinegar	45 mL
1 tbsp	Dijon mustard	15 mL
1 tsp	dried tarragon	5 mL
1/4 tsp	salt	1 mL
1/4 tsp	pepper	1 mL
1 cup	tiny whole mushrooms	250 mL
2	green onions, chopped	2
	Boston lettuce leaves	

1. Cut the chicken crosswise into strips 1/2 inch (1 cm) wide. Seed and core the red pepper; cut into strips. Cut broccoli into small florets; peel and cut stems into 1/4-inch (5 mm) thick slices.

2. In a large skillet, heat half the oil over medium-high heat. In 2 batches, add chicken; cook, stirring, for 6 minutes or until golden and no longer pink inside. Using a slotted spoon, transfer to a warmed bowl; cover and keep warm.

3. In the same skillet, heat remaining oil. Add red pepper and broccoli; cook for 2 minutes, stirring occasionally. Stir in stock and reduce heat to low; cover and steam for 2 minutes. Using a slotted spoon, add red pepper and broccoli to chicken.

Recipe continues...

SUGGESTED MENU

Skillet Chicken Salad

🐦

Carrot Sticks

🐦

Crusty Rolls

🐦

Applesauce and Cookies

EASY CHICKEN AND VEGETABLE STIR-FRY (PAGE 24) ➤
OVERLEAF: CHICKEN AND SPINACH SALAD WITH AVOCADO AND FRUIT (PAGE 74)

4. In the same skillet, bring vinegar to a boil, scraping up any brown bits from the bottom of the pan. Stir in mustard, tarragon, salt and pepper. Stir in mushrooms and onions. Return chicken mixture and any juices. Cook for a few seconds or until heated through.

5. Line 4 dinner plates with lettuce, top with the salad and serve.

≺ ROASTED CHICKEN FAJITAS (PAGE 38)

Curried Chicken and Pasta Salad

6	skinless boneless chicken breasts	6
1/4 cup	cider vinegar	50 mL
12 oz	medium shell pasta	375 g
8 oz	sugar snap or snow peas, trimmed	250 g
1	large red bell pepper, cut into thin strips	1
1/2 cup	coarsely chopped walnuts	125 mL
1/2 cup	seedless raisins	125 mL
1 1/2 cups	light mayonnaise	375 mL
1/2 cup	light sour cream	125 mL
4 tsp	curry powder, or to taste	20 mL
2 tsp	ground cumin	10 mL
	Salt and pepper	
	Lettuce leaves	

1. To poach chicken breasts, place in a shallow saucepan with vinegar and enough water to cover; bring to a simmer, cover, reduce heat to medium–low and cook for 15 to 20 minutes or until tender. Set aside to cool in poaching liquid.

2. Meanwhile, in a large pot of boiling salted water, cook pasta until tender but firm; drain. Rinse under cold water; drain well.

3. In a large saucepan of boiling water blanch peas for 1 minute. Refresh under cold running water and drain well; cool.

4. Cut the cooled cooked chicken into bite-sized pieces. In a large bowl, stir together chicken, pasta, peas, red pepper, walnuts and raisins.

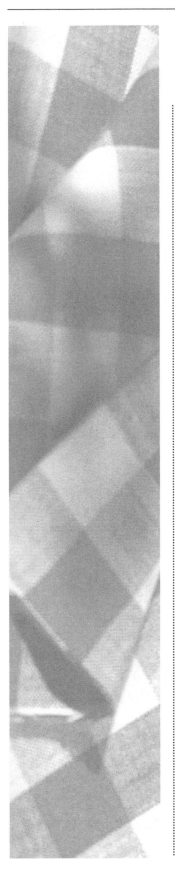

5. In a small bowl, stir together mayonnaise, sour cream, curry powder, cumin, and salt and pepper to taste. Stir gently into chicken mixture. Serve in a lettuce-lined bowl.

Caribbean Chicken Salad with Ginger-Lime Dressing

Tropical fruit and cooked chicken with a zesty lime dressing make a refreshing light main course for a hot summer day.

1/3 cup	light mayonnaise	75 mL
1/4 cup	light sour cream	50 mL
1 tsp	grated lime zest	5 mL
1/4 cup	fresh lime juice	50 mL
1 tbsp	minced ginger root	15 mL
2 1/2 cups	cubed cooked chicken	625 mL
1	mango or small papaya, peeled and cubed	1
1	can (14 oz [398 mL]) unsweetened pineapple chunks, drained	1
1/2 cup	sliced celery	125 mL
	Salt and pepper	
	Lettuce	
1/4 cup	toasted pecan halves	50 mL

1. In a large bowl, whisk together mayonnaise, sour cream, lime zest, lime juice and ginger.
2. Stir in chicken, mango, pineapple and celery. Season with salt and pepper to taste. Serve in lettuce-lined bowls or plates, sprinkled with pecan halves.

SUGGESTED MENU

Caribbean Chicken Salad with Ginger-Lime Dressing

Crusty Brown Rolls

Banana Bread

Thai Chicken–Noodle Salad

Garnish this pretty salad with julienned strips of unpeeled English cucumber and peeled mango for extra color and crunch.

SHOPPING TIPS

Chili paste, rice vermicelli and fish sauce are all available in Oriental supermarkets, and the first two are often found in regular supermarkets as well. Chili paste is bright red and made from chili peppers, salt and sometimes garlic. You can substitute hot pepper flakes. If you do not find rice vermicelli, another thin noodle will do. The rice vermicelli package instructs boiling the noodles for 3 minutes, but I find just soaking them in boiling water enough to soften them. Thai fish sauce is a staple for seasoning in that country. It has a salty taste and weird smell, but lends a wonderful and intriguing flavor to dishes. Seek it out; once you find it, store in the refrigerator for years!

4 oz	rice vermicelli	125 g
1	red bell pepper, cut into thin strips	1
2 cups	cooked chicken, cut into thin strips	500 mL
1 cup	shredded carrots	250 mL
1/2 cup	coarsely chopped fresh coriander	125 mL
1/2 cup	diagonally sliced green onions	125 mL
DRESSING		
1/4 cup	Thai fish sauce	50 mL
1/4 cup	fresh lime juice	50 mL
2 tbsp	packed brown sugar	25 mL
2 tsp	minced ginger root	10 mL
1	clove garlic, minced	1
1/2 tsp	bottled chili paste (or more to taste) *or* 1/4 tsp (1 mL) hot pepper flakes	2 mL

1. In a large heatproof bowl, cover rice noodles with boiling water; let stand for 5 minutes or until softened. Drain well.
2. In a large serving bowl, toss noodles together with pepper, chicken, carrots, coriander and green onions.
3. Dressing: In a small bowl, stir together fish sauce, lime juice, brown sugar, ginger, garlic and chili paste. Pour over noodle mixture and toss to coat well.

SUGGESTED MENU

Thai Chicken-Noodle Salad

🍂

★ Broiled Bananas

🍂

Ice Cream

★ *Broiled Bananas*
Peel bananas and cut lengthwise; arrange in shallow baking dish. Sprinkle with brown sugar, dot with butter and broil close to the element for 3 to 5 minutes, until golden brown. Serve with ice cream.

Chicken Caesar

Chicken joins everyone's favorite salad to turn it into a main course event—just right for a hot summer evening.

MAKE AHEAD

The dressing can be prepared, covered and refrigerated for up to 1 week.

SHOPPING TIPS

Croutons are available in many forms in the grocery store. Be sure they are fresh. It is easy to make your own by dicing Italian bread and sautéing it in a large skillet in olive oil with garlic until golden brown. For convenience, buy stir-fry chicken strips that are already cut.

DRESSING

1/2 cup	mayonnaise	125 mL
2	cloves garlic, minced	2
2 tbsp	fresh lemon juice	25 mL
2 tbsp	white wine vinegar	25 mL
2 tsp	Worcestershire sauce	10 mL
2 tsp	Dijon mustard	10 mL
2 tsp	anchovy paste	10 mL
	Black pepper	
4	slices bacon, diced	4
8 oz	skinless boneless chicken breasts, cut into 1/4-inch (5 mm) strips	250 g
1	head romaine lettuce, washed, dried and torn into bite-sized pieces	1
1 cup	croutons	250 mL
1/2 cup	freshly grated Parmesan cheese	125 mL

1. Dressing: In a small bowl, whisk together mayonnaise, garlic, lemon juice, vinegar, Worcestershire sauce, mustard, anchovy paste and pepper to taste. Cover and refrigerate.

2. In a large skillet, cook bacon over medium–high heat for 7 minutes or until crisp and brown; remove with slotted spoon to drain on paper towels. Pour off all but 1 tbsp (15 mL) drippings.

3. Heat drippings over medium–high heat and cook chicken, stirring often, for 5 minutes or until no longer pink inside.

SUGGESTED MENU

Chicken Caesar

❧

Sliced Tomatoes

❧

Brownies and
Ice Cream

4. Meanwhile, combine lettuce, croutons, half the bacon and half the cheese in a large salad bowl. Add cooked chicken. Stir together dressing and remaining cheese; pour over salad and toss to coat. Sprinkle with pepper and garnish with remaining bacon.

Grilled Chicken and Cheese Salad

SERVES 4

Barbecued chicken on simply dressed greens makes a quick warm main course salad.

SUGGESTED MENU

Grilled Chicken and Cheese Salad

↓

★ Tomato Salad Provençale

↓

Crusty Bread

↓

Sliced Fresh Peaches

★ *Tomato Salad Provençale*
Halve 2 tomatoes, scoop out seeds and place cut side up on a platter. Sprinkle with finely chopped black olives, diced celery and minced parsley. Drizzle with olive oil and lemon juice, and sprinkle with salt and pepper.

1/3 cup	olive oil	75 mL
2 tbsp	white wine vinegar	25 mL
3/4 tsp	chopped fresh marjoram or (1/4 tsp [1 mL]) dried	4 mL
3/4 tsp	chopped fresh sage or (1/4 tsp [1 mL]) dried	4 mL
1/2 tsp	salt	2 mL
1/4 tsp	pepper	1 mL
1 tbsp	Dijon mustard	15 mL
3	skinless boneless chicken breasts	3
6 cups	mixed torn greens	1.5 L
1 cup	shredded Swiss cheese	250 mL

1. In a small bowl, whisk together oil, vinegar, marjoram, sage, salt and pepper. In a large bowl, combine 2 tbsp (25 mL) of the oil mixture with the mustard. Add chicken, turning to coat thoroughly.

2. On a greased grill, cook chicken over medium-high heat for 12 to 15 minutes, turning once and brushing with any remaining mustard mixture, or until cooked through.

3. Meanwhile, toss the greens and cheese with remaining oil mixture and arrange on 4 dinner plates. Cut the cooked chicken into 1/2-inch (1 cm) thick strips and arrange on the salad.

Chicken Salad Niçoise

The classic version of this salad is made with tuna, but chicken makes a light, delicious variation for a hot summer day. Plan the night before to cook extra potatoes and beans. Don't let the long ingredient list put you off; the salad is quick and easy to make.

MAKE AHEAD

The dressing can be made up to 1 day ahead and refrigerated. Bring to room temperature and whisk to recombine before using. The salad ingredients can be tossed together (end of step 2) several hours ahead and refrigerated.

SUGGESTED MENU

Gazpacho
(or other chilled soup)

Chicken Salad Niçoise

Crusty Bread

Fresh Peaches and
Yogurt with Brown Sugar

GARLIC DRESSING

2	cloves garlic, crushed	2
2 tsp	Dijon mustard	10 mL
1/4 cup	fresh lemon juice	50 mL
1/2 cup	olive oil	125 mL
	Salt and pepper	
2 cups	shredded cooked chicken	500 mL
2 cups	cooked green beans, cut into 2-inch (5 cm) lengths	500 mL
6	small new potatoes, cooked and sliced	6
1	small red bell pepper, cut into strips	1
1	small red onion, thinly sliced	1
2 cups	sliced celery	500 mL
3/4 cup	black olives	175 mL
	Romaine lettuce, torn into bite-sized pieces	
3	hard-cooked eggs, quartered	3
4	tomatoes, cut into wedges	4

1. Garlic Dressing: In a small bowl, whisk together garlic, mustard and lemon juice. Gradually whisk in oil. Season to taste with salt and pepper. Set aside.

2. In a large bowl, combine chicken, beans, potatoes, red pepper, onion, celery and olives.

3. Pour dressing over chicken mixture and gently toss to coat. Line a shallow salad bowl with lettuce and spoon salad on top. Garnish with eggs and tomatoes.

Chicken and Spinach Salad with Avocado and Fruit

SERVES 4

The dressing on this salad is so delicious, you might want to double it to keep on hand in the refrigerator for future salads.

You can, of course, use cooked chicken left over from your Sunday roast. Three cups (750 mL) or so will do.

MAKE AHEAD

The dressing can be made, covered and refrigerated for up to 1 week. The chicken can be cooked, cooled, covered and refrigerated for up to 2 days.

SWEET-AND-SOUR DRESSING

1/4 cup	granulated sugar	50 mL
3 tbsp	white wine vinegar	45 mL
1 tsp	grated onion	5 mL
1/2 tsp	paprika	2 mL
1/2 tsp	dry mustard	2 mL
1/4 tsp	salt	1 mL
1/3 cup	vegetable oil	75 mL
8 oz	skinless boneless chicken breasts	250 g
Half	cantaloupe or other melon *or* 2 oranges, peeled and divided into segments	Half
8 oz	spinach, trimmed, washed, dried and torn into bite-sized pieces	250 g
1	avocado, peeled and thinly sliced	1
	Salt and pepper	

1. Sweet-and-Sour Dressing: In a small saucepan over medium heat, combine sugar and vinegar; cook, stirring, for 2 minutes or until the sugar dissolves. Cool. Stir in onion, paprika, mustard and salt. Transfer mixture to a blender; with motor running, add oil in a slow stream through the feed tube.

2. Meanwhile, put chicken in a saucepan with 1/4 inch (5 mm) water and bring to a boil. Reduce heat to medium-low; cover and simmer, turning once, for 5 minutes or until just cooked through. Remove chicken, cool and cut crosswise into 1/4-inch (5 mm) slices.

SUGGESTED MENU

Chicken and Spinach Salad with Avocado and Fruit

Crusty Bread

Corn on the Cob

Brownies

3. Scoop out melon with melon baller or cut into cubes. In a large salad bowl, toss spinach, chicken, avocado, melon, dressing, and salt and pepper to taste.

Oven Roasts and Broils

This simple, but delicious recipe produces moist chicken with nice crisp skin and is easily halved or doubled.

Chicken Breasts with Chili Butter

PREHEAT OVEN TO 400° F (200° C)

1/4 cup	unsalted butter, softened	50 mL
1 tbsp	chili powder	15 mL
1/2 tsp	salt	2 mL
1/4 tsp	hot pepper flakes	1 mL
2	cloves garlic, minced	2
4	bone-in skin-on chicken breasts	4

1. In a small bowl, cream together butter, chili powder, salt, hot pepper flakes and garlic until well blended. Divide into 4 portions.

2. Gently poke your fingers under the skin of each breast and lift the skin slightly. Being careful not to tear the membrane that connects the skin to the chicken, gently stuff one portion of the chili butter between, massaging to even out.

3. Arrange breasts skin-side up on a rack in a large shallow roasting pan. Roast in preheated oven for 30 minutes or until chicken is no longer pink inside, brushing once or twice with melted butter from the bottom of the pan.

Moroccan Baked Chicken

SERVES 4

Chicken is often on the menus in Morocco — but always enlivened with wonderful spice combinations.

SUGGESTED MENU

Moroccan Baked Chicken

❧

Couscous

❧

★ Carrot and Zucchini Sauté

❧

★ Broiled Cinnamon Pears with Honeyed Yogurt

★ Carrot and Zucchini Sauté
Cook carrot and zucchini slices in olive oil until tender-crisp, for 3 to 5 minutes, stirring often. Season with salt and pepper to taste, and stir in chopped fresh parsley to serve.

★ Broiled Cinnamon Pears
Place pear halves, cut side up, in a baking dish; dot with butter, sprinkle with cinnamon and broil until golden brown and tender, for about 10 minutes. Serve warm with yogurt sweetened to taste with liquid honey.

PREHEAT OVEN TO 425° F (220° C)
FOIL-LINED BAKING SHEET

1/2 cup	packed parsley	125 mL
1/2 cup	fresh coriander leaves	125 mL
1/4 cup	fresh lemon juice	50 mL
2 tsp	paprika	10 mL
2 tsp	ground cumin	10 mL
1/4 tsp	hot pepper flakes	1 mL
1/4 tsp	cinnamon	1 mL
2	cloves garlic	2
1/4 cup	olive oil	50 mL
	Salt and pepper	
4	skinless boneless chicken breasts, 4 diagonal slits (each 1/2 inch [1 cm]) cut on smooth side of each breast	4
	Hot couscous	

1. In a food processor, chop parsley and coriander. Add lemon juice, paprika, cumin, hot pepper flakes and cinnamon; with the motor running, drop garlic through the feed tube; process until finely chopped. Transfer to a bowl; whisk in the oil. Set aside 1 tbsp (15 mL) of parsley mixture.

2. Sprinkle each breast with salt and pepper; coat with the parsley mixture and place in a single layer on pre-pared baking sheet. Bake in preheated oven for 20 to 25 minutes or until chicken is no longer pink inside.

3. Serve on a bed of hot couscous; top with reserved parsley mixture.

Crisp Coconut Chicken with Mango Salsa

SERVES 2

This delicious chicken stays moist under its crisp coating, which happily teams up with a tropical-flavored sauce.

SHOPPING TIP

To tell when a mango is ripe, squeeze it gently with your hands. The mango should give slightly and not feel hard. A ripe mango is also the most aromatic.

SUGGESTED MENU

Crisp Coconut Chicken with Mango Salsa

Rice

Stir-Fried Snow Peas and Red Bell Pepper Strips

★ Bananas Baked with Rum

★ Bananas Baked with Rum
Halve bananas lengthwise and place, cut-side down, in a shallow baking dish. Sprinkle with brown sugar, drizzle with rum and dot with butter. Bake in a 400° F (200° C) oven for about 10 minutes while you enjoy your main course.

PREHEAT OVEN TO 375° F (190° C)

1	clove garlic, crushed	1
1 tbsp	Dijon mustard	15 mL
Pinch	ground ginger	Pinch
2	skinless boneless chicken breasts	2
	All-purpose flour	
1/4 tsp	salt	1 mL
1/4 tsp	pepper	1 mL
1	egg	1
3/4 cup	sweetened flaked coconut	175 mL
1 tbsp	vegetable oil	15 mL
2 tbsp	fresh lime juice	25 mL

MANGO SALSA

1	ripe mango, diced	1
1/4 cup	diced red onions	50 mL
1 tbsp	fresh lime juice *or* white wine vinegar	15 mL
1 tbsp	chopped fresh coriander or parsley	15 mL
	Salt and pepper	
Pinch	hot pepper flakes	Pinch

1. In a small bowl, combine garlic, mustard and ginger; spread mixture lightly on both sides of each chicken breast. Place chicken on waxed paper and sprinkle both sides lightly with flour, salt and pepper.

2. In a shallow bowl, stir egg together with 1 tsp (5 mL) cold water. Place coconut on waxed paper. Dip chicken breasts in egg wash, then in the coconut, pressing to make it adhere.

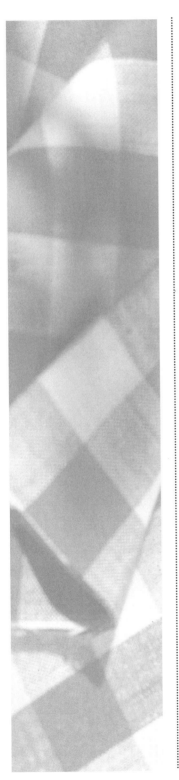

3. In an ovenproof skillet, heat oil over medium-high heat. Add chicken and cook for 2 minutes a side. Add lime juice to the skillet and place in preheated oven for 12 to 15 minutes or until the chicken is no longer pink inside.

4. Salsa: Meanwhile, in a bowl combine mango, red onions, lime juice and coriander. Season to taste with salt and pepper. Stir in hot pepper flakes.

5. Divide salsa between 2 dinner plates and place the cooked chicken on top.

Genie's Cranberry Chicken

SERVES 8

This wonderful company dish is adapted from a recipe by my Cambridge friend, Genie Berger, who loves cranberries as much as I do.

SUGGESTED MENU

Cranberry Chicken

★ White and Wild Rice

Green Peas

Mashed Rutabaga

★ Apple Tart

★ White and Wild Rice
On the supermarket shelves, there are some good commercial mixes of the two rices that take only 20 minutes of cooking.

★ Apple Tart
Sauté apple slices in butter and sugar until almost soft. Arrange on a puff pastry rectangle; sprinkle with Calvados or cider and while you enjoy the main course, bake in 400° F (200° C) oven for about 20 minutes. Enjoy warm. (You'll need a half package [411 g] puff pastry, thawed.)

PREHEAT OVEN TO 375° F (190° C)
13- BY 9-INCH (3 L) BAKING DISH, GREASED

8	bone-in skin-on chicken breasts, patted dry	8
2 tbsp	vegetable oil	25 mL
12 oz	cranberries, fresh or frozen	375 g
1/3 cup	granulated sugar	75 mL
2 tbsp	cornstarch	25 mL
1/2 cup	mild liquid honey	125 mL
2 tsp	fresh lemon juice	10 mL
	Salt and pepper	
1/4 cup	orange liqueur *or* orange juice	50 mL
1 tbsp	grated orange zest	15 mL

1. In a large skillet, heat oil over medium-high heat. Add chicken in batches and cook until browned on all sides.

2. Meanwhile, sprinkle cranberries in prepared baking dish. Combine sugar and cornstarch and spread over the cranberries. Drizzle with honey and lemon juice. Place in preheated oven while the chicken browns.

3. Remove baking dish from oven and arrange chicken on top of cranberry mixture. Sprinkle with salt and pepper, orange liqueur and zest. Bake for 30 minutes or until chicken is no longer pink inside, covering with foil if chicken or cranberries get too brown. Remove chicken to a warm platter; stir cranberry sauce well and spoon over top.

Sesame Chicken Fingers with Honey Dip

Kids will love eating these "fingers" with their fingers; so why not make a whole meal of finger food, using the dip for raw vegetables as well.

MAKE AHEAD

The chicken fingers and the honey dip can be made up to 4 hours ahead, covered and refrigerated.

SUGGESTED MENU

Sesame Chicken Fingers with Honey Dip

Raw Vegetable Sticks (Carrot, cucumber, celery, rutabaga)

★ Oven Fries

Ice Cream and Cookies

★ Oven Fries
(Prepare and place in the oven before the chicken.) Cut 3 large scrubbed but unpeeled baking potatoes into 12 wedges each. Toss with 1/2 tsp (2 mL) paprika and 1 tbsp (15 mL) vegetable oil; spread out in a single layer on a baking sheet. Bake in a 400° F (200° C) oven for 15 minutes; turn and bake for 15 minutes longer or until the potatoes are crisp and golden brown. Sprinkle with salt and serve hot.

PREHEAT OVEN TO 400° F (200° C)
FOIL-LINED COOKIE SHEET, GREASED

HONEY DIP

1/3 cup	light mayonnaise	75 mL
3 tbsp	liquid honey	45 mL
1 tbsp	fresh lemon juice	15 mL
1/4 cup	light mayonnaise	50 mL
2 tbsp	Dijon mustard	25 mL
2 tbsp	fresh lemon juice	25 mL
1/3 cup	dry bread crumbs	75 mL
3 tbsp	sesame seeds	45 mL
1 tsp	dried Italian herb seasoning	5 mL
1 lb	skinless boneless chicken breasts cut into fingers, 2 inches (5 cm) long by 1/2 inch (1 cm) wide	500 g

1. Honey Dip: In a small bowl, stir together the 1/3 cup (75 mL) mayonnaise, honey and 1 tbsp (15 mL) lemon juice until well combined. Refrigerate if making ahead.

2. In a small bowl, combine the 1/4 cup (50 mL) mayonnaise, Dijon mustard and 2 tbsp (25 mL) lemon juice.

3. On waxed paper or in a shallow bowl, combine the bread crumbs, sesame seeds and Italian seasoning.

4. Coat chicken with mayonnaise mixture, then with bread crumb mixture. Place on prepared cookie sheet. Bake in preheated oven for 15 to 20 minutes or until golden brown and the chicken is no longer pink inside, turning once. Serve hot with the honey dip.

Quick Chicken and Mushroom Pot Pies

One of my favorite uses for chicken left from Sunday's roast is a pot pie, and I couldn't resist including one here, even though it meant cheating and baking the pastry separately.

SHOPPING TIP

Brown mushrooms, often the same price as white, are more flavorful.

SUGGESTED MENU

Quick Chicken and Mushroom Pot Pies

Chili Sauce

Green Salad

★ Raisin Baked Apples

★ Raisin Baked Apples
Fill cored apples with a mixture of raisins, brown sugar, butter, cinnamon and cloves; drizzle with apple cider and bake, uncovered and basting often, in 400° F (200° C) oven for about 30 minutes or until tender.

PREHEAT OVEN TO 400° F (200° C)

Half	pkg (14 oz [411 g]) puff pastry, thawed	Half
1	egg, beaten	1
2 tbsp	butter	25 mL
8 oz	small mushrooms	250 g
2	carrots, peeled and sliced	2
1	stalk celery, sliced	1
1	onion, chopped	1
1/4 tsp	dried thyme	1 mL
1/4 tsp	dried rosemary	1 mL
1 1/2 cups	chicken stock	375 mL
2 tbsp	cornstarch	25 mL
3 cups	cooked chicken, cut into small pieces	750 mL
1 cup	frozen peas	250 mL
2 tbsp	chopped fresh parsley	25 mL
	Salt and pepper	

1. Roll out enough puff pastry to cut 4 circles slightly bigger than the tops of 4 deep soup bowls. Cut out the circles and place on a cookie sheet; brush with egg and bake in preheated oven for 15 to 20 minutes or until puffed and golden brown.

2. Meanwhile, in a large saucepan, melt butter over medium heat. Add mushrooms, carrots, celery and onion; cook for 5 minutes. Stir in thyme, rosemary and 1 cup (250 mL) of the stock; bring to a boil. Dissolve the cornstarch in remaining stock and stir into vegetable mixture; cook, stirring, until thickened.

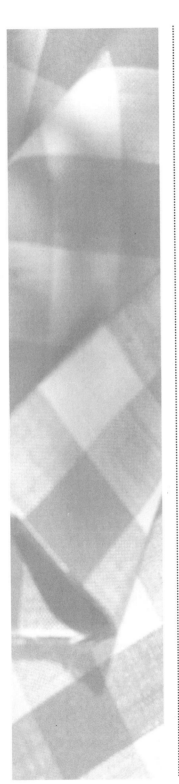

3. Stir in the chicken, peas and parsley. Season to taste with salt and pepper. Transfer to warm soup bowls and top each with a hot pastry round to serve.

Quick-Roasted Lemon Thighs

SERVES 3

If you wish, you can substitute 3 bone-in breasts for the thighs in this simple and easy recipe that creates a wonderfully crisp skin and moist meat.

SUGGESTED MENU

Quick-Roasted Lemon Thighs

❧

★ Parmesan Oven Fries

❧

Sautéed Zucchini and Red Bell Pepper Slices

❧

Fresh Fruit

★ *Parmesan Oven Fries*
Toss sliced potatoes with olive oil, Parmesan cheese and pepper; spread out on a cookie sheet and bake in 425° F (220° C) oven for 30 minutes, turning once.

PREHEAT OVEN TO 425° F (220° C)
FOIL-LINED ROASTING PAN

6	chicken thighs	6
2	cloves garlic	2
3 tbsp	fresh lemon juice	45 mL
1 tbsp	Worcestershire sauce	15 mL
1/2 tsp	salt	2 mL

1. Place chicken thighs in a glass dish just big enough to hold them in a single layer.

2. In a blender or mini chopper, combine garlic, lemon juice and Worcestershire sauce; purée until smooth. Coat chicken with mixture and leave at room temperature for 15 minutes.

3. Arrange chicken on a rack in prepared roasting pan; sprinkle with salt. Roast in preheated oven for about 30 minutes or until chicken is no longer pink inside.

Easy Tandoori Chicken

SERVES 4

A spicy paste is rubbed on and under the skin, and the chicken is broiled close to the element or grilled over high heat to make it crisp and flavorful. Real tandoori chicken is marinated in yogurt and spices, then roasted in a *tandoor*, which reaches incredibly high temperatures.

SUGGESTED MENU

Easy Tandoori Chicken

❧

Cold Plain Yogurt

❧

Mango Chutney

❧

Rice

❧

Green Peas

❧

Sautéed Eggplant Slices

❧

Lemon Ice

PREHEAT BROILER
BROILER PAN WITH GREASED RACK

2 tbsp	fresh lemon juice	25 mL
1 tbsp	minced ginger root	15 mL
3	cloves garlic, minced	3
1/4 tsp	ground allspice	1 mL
1/4 tsp	cinnamon	1 mL
1/4 tsp	black pepper	1 mL
1/4 tsp	cayenne pepper	1 mL
4	chicken legs with thighs attached	4

1. In a bowl combine lemon juice, ginger, garlic, allspice, cinnamon, black pepper and cayenne; mix to form a paste. Loosen skin of each thigh by slipping your fingers between the skin and the flesh and over the thigh-leg joint. Spread 3/4 tsp (4 mL) of the paste on the flesh and squeeze to distribute evenly. Spread the remainder over the outside surfaces.

2. Place chicken skin-side down in prepared pan. Broil about 6 inches (15 cm) from the heat for 15 minutes. Turn the pieces over and broil 10 to 15 minutes longer or until meat near the thighbone is no longer pink inside, placing a piece of foil, shiny side up, on top if the chicken gets too brown. (Alternatively, place skin-side up on greased grill and barbecue, turning after 15 minutes.)

Oven-Barbecued Chicken

SERVES 4

The rich tomato flavor of this oven dish will appeal to the whole family. If you wish to cut down on the fat in this already low-fat supper, remove the skin from the chicken. (The sauce will keep it from drying out.)

MAKE AHEAD

The sauce can be made several hours ahead, covered and refrigerated. Heat, stirring, before spooning over chicken.

SUGGESTED MENU

Oven-Barbecued
Chicken

Mashed Potatoes

Baked Winter Squash

Green Peas

⬥

Applesauce and
Cookies

PREHEAT OVEN TO 450° F (230° C)
13- BY 9-INCH (3 L) BAKING DISH, GREASED

2 1/2 lbs	chicken pieces, such as bone-in breasts, thighs, and/or drumsticks	1.25 kg
	Salt and pepper	
1 tbsp	vegetable oil	15 mL
1	onion, finely chopped	1
3/4 cup	ketchup	175 mL
1/4 cup	cider vinegar	50 mL
1 tbsp	Worcestershire sauce	15 mL
1 tbsp	packed brown sugar	15 mL
1 tsp	dry mustard	5 mL
Dash	Tabasco sauce	Dash

1. Arrange chicken in a single layer in prepared baking dish. Sprinkle with salt and pepper.

2. In a large skillet, heat oil over medium heat. Add onion and cook, stirring, for 5 minutes. Stir in ketchup, vinegar, Worcestershire sauce, brown sugar, dry mustard and Tabasco to taste. Bring sauce to a boil, stirring.

3. Spoon sauce evenly over chicken pieces and bake in the preheated oven for 20 to 30 minutes or until chicken is no longer pink inside.

Broiled Rosemary Thighs

This very simple recipe creates wonderfully moist and delicious chicken.

MAKE AHEAD

The chicken can be marinated, covered and refrigerated, for up to 4 hours. Bring to room temperature for 30 minutes before cooking.

SUGGESTED MENU

Broiled Rosemary Thighs

★ Salad of Mozzarella and Tomato Slices with Basil Vinaigrette

Italian Bread

Peaches and Cream

★ Salad of Mozzarella and Tomato Slices with Basil Vinaigrette
Alternate fresh mozzarella slices overlapping with tomato slices on a platter. Add chopped fresh basil to a mustard vinaigrette of 1/3 cup (75 mL) olive oil, 1 tbsp (15 mL) wine vinegar, 1 tsp (5 mL) Dijon mustard, and salt and pepper to taste; drizzle over the salad.

PREHEAT BROILER
FOIL-LINED BROILING PAN

8	chicken thighs	8
3 tbsp	fresh lemon juice	45 mL
3 tbsp	olive oil	45 mL
1 tbsp	chopped fresh rosemary (or 1 tsp [5 mL] crumbled dried)	15 mL
1/2 tsp	grated lemon zest	2 mL
	Salt and pepper	

1. Place chicken thighs in a glass dish just big enough to hold them in a single layer. In a bowl whisk together the lemon juice, olive oil, rosemary and lemon zest. Pour over chicken and turn to coat well. Cover and let stand at room temperature for 30 minutes.

2. Reserving the marinade, arrange chicken thighs skin-side down on prepared pan; sprinkle with salt and pepper. Broil 4 inches (10 cm) from heat for 7 minutes, basting occasionally.

3. Turn, baste and broil 5 to 8 minutes longer, or until chicken is no longer pink inside.

Baked Herb and Cheese Stuffed Breasts

PREHEAT OVEN TO 400° F (200° C)
SHALLOW BAKING DISH, GREASED

6	skinless boneless chicken breasts	6
	Salt and pepper	
6	thin slices prosciutto	6
	Olive oil	
1 tbsp	dried Italian herb seasoning	15 mL
1/4 lb	Fontina cheese	125 g
1	egg	1
1/3 cup	all-purpose flour	75 mL
1/2 cup	dry bread crumbs	125 mL

1. Place chicken breasts between 2 pieces of plastic wrap and pound to an even thickness of about 1/8 inch (3 mm). Sprinkle with salt and pepper. Lay a piece of prosciutto on each. Brush with olive oil and sprinkle some of the herbs on each, using 2 tsp (10 mL) for the 6 breasts. Cut the cheese lengthwise into 6 pieces and place a piece crosswise on each chicken breast. Roll up to enclose the cheese.

2. In a small bowl, beat egg with 1 tbsp (15 mL) olive oil. Place flour on waxed paper or in a bowl. Stir together remaining herbs and bread crumbs in another bowl. Coat each breast in flour, then dip in egg and roll in crumbs to coat.

3. Arrange stuffed breasts in prepared baking dish. Brush with olive oil and sprinkle with salt and pepper. Bake in preheated oven for about 25 minutes or until golden brown and the chicken is no longer pink inside.

Baked Chutney Chicken

SERVES 3 OR 4

This quick and easy dish is so delicious you'll keep mango chutney on hand to make it often. It doesn't matter what kind you buy.

SUGGESTED MENU

Baked Chutney Chicken

Rice

★ Baked Carrots

★ Minted Green Peas

Fruit Salad

★ *Baked Carrots*
Place sliced carrots in a casserole; sprinkle with sugar, salt and pepper. Dot with butter, cover and bake for 30 minutes in 400° F (200° C) oven.

★ *Minted Peas*
Add finely chopped fresh mint or a pinch of dried mint to cooked peas.

PREHEAT OVEN TO 400° F (200° C)

1 tbsp	vegetable oil	15 mL
6 to 8	chicken thighs, patted dry	6 to 8
	Salt and pepper	
1/2 cup	mango chutney	125 mL
1 tbsp	soya sauce	15 mL
1 tbsp	red wine vinegar	15 mL

1. In a large ovenproof skillet, heat oil over medium-high heat. Add thighs, skin-side down; cook for 5 minutes or until the skin is crisp. Remove chicken and drain off all the fat. Return chicken to skillet, skin-side up; sprinkle with salt and pepper.

2. Meanwhile, chop any big bits of chutney; stir it together with the soya sauce and vinegar. Spoon over chicken and bake, uncovered, in preheated oven for 15 to 20 minutes or until chicken is no longer pink inside.

Greek-Style Baked Chicken

This dish is so colorful and delicious no one will know how easy and quick it is to prepare. Garnish it with some black olives if you wish.

SUGGESTED MENU

Greek-Style Baked Chicken

Green Beans

★ Greek Potatoes or Rice

Purchased Baklava or Fresh Fruit

★ Greek Potatoes
Quarter 6 small potatoes and parboil in salted water for 10 minutes. Drain well and toss in baking pan with 2 tbsp (25 mL) butter, 1/3 cup (75 mL) fresh lemon juice and 1 tsp (5 mL) dried oregano. Bake, uncovered, for 20 to 25 minutes until tender in 400° F (200° C) oven with the chicken.

PREHEAT OVEN TO 400° F (200° C)
BAKING DISH, GREASED

4	small skinless boneless chicken breasts	4
	Black pepper	
2	small tomatoes (preferably plum), diced	2
2 tbsp	diced red or yellow bell pepper	25 mL
2 tbsp	chopped fresh parsley	25 mL
1/2 tsp	dried oregano	2 mL
2	cloves garlic, minced	2
1 cup	crumbled feta cheese	250 mL
1 tbsp	olive oil	15 mL

1. Arrange chicken breasts in a greased baking dish just big enough to hold them in a single layer. Sprinkle with pepper and set aside.

2. In a bowl, toss together tomatoes, bell pepper, parsley, oregano, garlic and feta cheese. Spoon over chicken, drizzle with olive oil and bake in preheated oven for 25 to 30 minutes or until chicken is no longer pink inside.

Julia Aitken's Orange-Thyme Chicken with Honey Glaze

SERVES 3

This lovely idea of tucking herbs and citrus zest under the skin of chicken comes from my good friend, Julia Aitken, the food editor of *Elm Street*. I've adapted it from a recipe that originally appeared in the magazine. You can also use chicken breasts, allowing for a longer roasting time.

SUGGESTED MENU

Orange-Thyme Chicken
with Honey Glaze

Sweet Potato Slices

Brussels Sprouts or
Broccoli

★ Sautéed Apple Slices
over Vanilla Ice Cream

★ Sautéed Apple Slices
Toss 4 sliced apples with the juice and zest of 1 lemon and 1/2 cup (125 mL) granulated sugar. Cook in butter in a skillet until soft but still holding their shape; sprinkle with cinnamon and serve warm over ice cream.

PREHEAT OVEN TO **400° F (200° C)**

1 tbsp	grated orange zest	15 mL
2 tsp	dried thyme	10 mL
6	skin-on chicken thighs, patted dry	6
1 tbsp	olive oil	15 mL
1/2 tsp	salt	2 mL
1/4 tsp	pepper	1 mL
1/4 cup	fresh orange juice	50 mL
2 tbsp	liquid honey	25 mL

1. In a small bowl, mix together orange zest and thyme; divide mixture into 6 portions. Gently loosen skin from each thigh and push a portion of the orange zest mixture between the skin and the meat of each thigh.

2. In a large ovenproof skillet, heat oil over medium-high heat. Add thighs, skin-side down; cook for 5 minutes or until the skin is crisp. Remove chicken and drain off all the fat. Return chicken back to skillet, skin-side up. Sprinkle with salt and pepper.

3. Meanwhile, in a bowl stir together orange juice and honey. Spoon half of mixture over chicken and bake, uncovered, in preheated oven for 10 minutes. Spoon remaining mixture over thighs and bake for another 5 to 10 minutes or until chicken is no longer pink inside.

Mango and Brie-Stuffed Breasts

Fruit and cheese make up the filling for these special chicken rolls. They're perfect for entertaining.

MAKE AHEAD

The rolls can be completely prepared to the end of step 2, covered and refrigerated for up to 4 hours. Bring to room temperature for 30 minutes before cooking.

SUGGESTED MENU

Mango and Brie-Stuffed Breasts

Buttered Basmati Rice

Steamed Asparagus

★ Mustard Broiled Tomatoes

Sorbet and Cookies

★ Mustard Broiled Tomatoes
Spread tomato halves with Dijon mustard and sprinkle with pepper. When you remove the chicken from the oven, broil tomatoes for 3 to 5 minutes until softened.

PREHEAT OVEN TO 400° F (200° C)

4	skinless boneless chicken breasts	4
1	mango, peeled and sliced into long thin wedges	1
4 oz	Brie cheese	125 g
1/4 cup	all-purpose flour	50 mL
1/2 tsp	dried thyme	2 mL
	Salt and pepper	
2 tbsp	butter	25 mL
2 tbsp	balsamic or wine vinegar	25 mL
1 cup	chicken stock	250 mL

1. Place breasts between 2 pieces of plastic wrap and pound to an even thickness of about 1/8 inch (3 mm). Arrange mango slices down the center of each breast. Cut Brie lengthwise into 4 pieces and place a piece on each breast. Roll up each breast to enclose the filling. If needed, secure with bamboo skewers or tie with string.

2. In a small shallow bowl, combine flour, thyme, 1/2 tsp (2 mL) salt and 1/4 tsp (1 mL) pepper. Roll chicken in mixture to coat.

3. In a large ovenproof skillet, melt butter over medium-high heat. Cook chicken rolls, turning, for 5 to 7 minutes or until browned on all sides. Bake in preheated oven for 20 minutes or until no longer pink inside. Transfer to a plate to keep warm. If necessary, remove any skewers or string before serving.

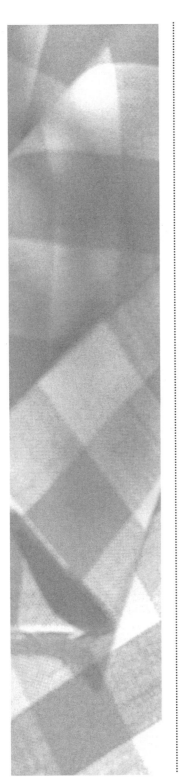

4. Stir vinegar into skillet and bring to a boil over high heat, scraping up any bits on the bottom. Add stock and bring to a boil. Reduce heat and simmer, uncovered, for about 5 minutes or until reduced by nearly half. Pour over the chicken.

Broiled Chicken and Squash

Broiling is a fast way to cook a whole chicken and it ensures crisp skin and juicy meat.

MAKE AHEAD

Both the chicken and squash can be prepared, covered and refrigerated up to 1 day ahead. Bring to room temperature for 30 minutes before cooking.

SHOPPING TIP

Occasionally, you can find squash pre-cut into rings in the produce department; or, you can do this a day ahead, popping the rings into a plastic bag in the crisper.

SUGGESTED MENU

Broiled Chicken and Squash

Green Salad

Crusty Bread

Fresh Pineapple Rings

PREHEAT BROILER
BROILING PAN WITH GREASED RACK

1	broiler or frying chicken (about 3 lbs [1.5 kg])	1
1	lemon	1
1 tbsp	Dijon mustard	15 mL
1/4 cup	Olive oil	50 mL
1	acorn squash	1

1. Place chicken on a cutting board, breast-side down. Remove backbone with poultry shears by cutting as close as possible to the bone on either side. Turn the chicken over and flatten it as much as possible with your hand. Break the joints so the chicken lies flat. (Or, ask your butcher to "butterfly" a chicken for you.)

2. Grate zest from the lemon. In a bowl combine zest with mustard; spread mixture over both sides of the chicken. Squeeze juice from the lemon and combine with oil; brush over the chicken, reserving any remainder. Place bone-side up in prepared pan.

3. Scrub the squash well and cut into 1-inch (2.5 cm) rings, removing the seeds. Arrange to one side of the chicken and cover with a piece of foil.

4. Place pan 4 inches (10 cm) from heat and broil for 15 minutes, brushing once with the remaining lemon mixture. Using tongs, carefully turn the chicken over. Remove foil from squash rings. Brush both chicken and squash well with the lemon mixture. Broil for 10 or 15 minutes, brushing once or twice more, and turning the squash once. (If the squash is tender before the chicken is done, remove and keep warm.) The chicken is done when it is no longer pink inside.

CRISP COCONUT CHICKEN WITH MANGO SALSA (PAGE 80) ➤
OVERLEAF: HONEY-GARLIC CHICKEN WINGS (PAGE 30)

Orange-Rosemary Glazed Chicken Breasts

This easy chicken, with its fresh citrus and herb flavor, is moist and delicious when cooked at high heat.

SUGGESTED MENU

Orange-Rosemary
Glazed Chicken Breasts

❧

Sweet Potato Slices

❧

Asparagus or Green Peas

❧

Raspberries and Cream

PREHEAT OVEN TO 500° F (260° C)
FOIL-LINED PAN

1/2 cup	frozen orange juice concentrate	125 mL
2 tbsp	fresh lemon juice	25 mL
4 tsp	minced fresh rosemary (or 1 tsp [5 mL] crumbled dried)	20 mL
1 tsp	pepper	5 mL
4	skin-on bone-in chicken breasts	4

1. In a small saucepan, combine orange concentrate, lemon juice, rosemary and pepper; cook over medium-low heat until the concentrate is melted.

2. Arrange chicken breasts skin-side down in prepared pan. Brush with some of the orange mixture. Roast in preheated oven for 15 minutes, basting once with the orange mixture.

3. Turn chicken and baste liberally with orange mixture. Roast for about 15 minutes longer or until chicken is no longer pink inside, basting once more with the orange mixture and covering with foil if the skin gets too brown.

◄ BASQUE DRUMSTICKS (PAGE 106)

Grilled Chicken with Corn Sauce

There's something so comforting about cream corn, and here it becomes the sauce for simple broiled or barbecued chicken breasts. This idea came from my assistant, Sharon Boyd. She loves cream corn too.

4	skinless boneless chicken breasts	4
2 tbsp	vegetable oil	25 mL
1 tsp	dried basil	5 mL
2	cloves garlic, minced	2
1/4 tsp	pepper	1 mL
1/4 tsp	hot pepper flakes	1 mL
2	green onions, sliced	2
1	red bell pepper, diced	1
1	can (14 oz [398 mL]) cream corn	1

1. Brush chicken breasts with half the oil. In a bowl combine basil, half the garlic, the pepper and hot pepper flakes. Rub mixture over the chicken and broil close to the heat (or over medium–high heat on the barbecue) for 5 to 6 minutes per side, turning once, until the chicken is no longer pink inside.

2. Meanwhile, in a skillet, heat the remaining oil over medium heat. Add onions, the remaining garlic and red pepper; cook for 5 minutes. Add corn; cook, stirring often, until hot and bubbly. Spoon over the chicken.

SUGGESTED MENU

Grilled Chicken with
Corn Sauce
❧
Mashed Potatoes
❧
Steamed Broccoli
❧
Brown Rolls
❧
Applesauce and
Cookies

Crisp Herbed Baked Chicken

SERVES 4

This easy baked chicken has a flavorful and crunchy coating that keeps the interior nice and moist. If you wish, substitute 8 thighs and bake for 5 minutes or so longer. Use whatever mustard you have on hand. Sometimes I just use the regular ballpark hot dog stuff.

MAKE AHEAD

The chicken can be coated, covered and refrigerated for up to 4 hours. Bring to room temperature 30 minutes before baking.

PREHEAT OVEN TO 400° F (200° C)
FOIL-LINED BAKING SHEET, GREASED

2 cups	corn cereal flakes	500 mL
1/4 cup	freshly grated Parmesan cheese	50 mL
1/4 tsp	pepper	1 mL
1/4 cup	light mayonnaise	50 mL
1 tbsp	prepared mustard	15 mL
1 tsp	dried Italian herb seasoning	5 mL
4	skinless boneless chicken breasts	4

1. With a rolling pin, crush corn flakes in a sealed plastic bag. Add cheese and pepper; shake to combine.
2. In a shallow dish, stir together mayonnaise, mustard and herb seasoning.
3. Dip each breast in mayonnaise mixture, then shake in the crumb mixture to coat. Arrange coated chicken breasts on prepared baking sheet. Bake in preheated oven for 20 to 25 minutes or until golden brown on the outside and it is no longer pink inside.

★ *Oven Fries*
Toss thinly sliced potatoes with olive oil to coat, 2 tbsp (25 mL) Parmesan cheese and 1 tbsp (15 mL) lemon juice. Spread out on a baking sheet and bake in 400° F (200° C) oven for about 30 minutes.

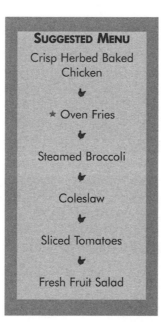

SUGGESTED MENU

Crisp Herbed Baked Chicken

❧

★ Oven Fries

❧

Steamed Broccoli

❧

Coleslaw

❧

Sliced Tomatoes

❧

Fresh Fruit Salad

Knife-and-Fork Chicken and Avocado Sandwich

Long, slender rolls (like braided poppy seed) are best to show off the layers of color in this delicious knife-and-fork hot sandwich. With a bowl of soup, it makes a quick and fun supper. Butter the rolls if you wish.

If fresh hot chili peppers are not available, substitute about 1/4 tsp (1 mL) hot pepper flakes, or to taste.

SUGGESTED MENU

Corn Chowder

Knife-and-Fork Chicken and Avocado Sandwich

★ Cinnamon Bananas with Honey Yogurt (see recipe, page 138)

3 tbsp	fresh lime juice	45 mL
1 tbsp	vegetable oil	15 mL
1/2 tsp	black pepper	2 mL
1/4 tsp	dried oregano	1 mL
4	skinless boneless chicken breasts	4
1	avocado	1
2	tomatoes	2
2 tsp	finely chopped fresh hot chili pepper	10 mL
1 tbsp	finely chopped red onion	15 mL
4	rolls, sliced lengthwise	4
2 cups	shredded Monterey Jack or mild Cheddar cheese	500 mL

1. In a bowl stir together 2 tbsp (25 mL) lime juice, oil, black pepper and oregano. Add chicken, turning to coat well. Cover and marinate at room temperature for 30 minutes.

2. Reserving marinade, remove chicken to broiler pan and broil 6 inches (15 cm) from heat, turning once and brushing with reserved marinade, for 8 to 10 minutes or until no longer pink inside. Transfer to a plate; cover and keep warm.

3. Lightly toast rolls, cut-side up, under broiler.

4. Meanwhile, peel and halve avocado lengthwise; remove pit. In a small bowl, mash half the avocado. Dice 1 tomato and stir into mashed avocado with remaining lime juice, chili pepper and onion. Slice remaining avocado and tomato.

5. Slice chicken into thin slices on diagonal. Spread 4 bottom halves of rolls with mashed avocado mixture; top with chicken. Layer with avocado and tomato slices, pressing down lightly. Top with cheese. Broil for 2 minutes or until cheese melts. Serve with top halves of rolls.

Spicy Roasted Drumsticks or Wings

SERVES 4

You probably already have everything in the cupboard for the zesty coating in this simple chicken recipe.

MAKE AHEAD

Drumsticks can be coated with mustard mixture, covered and refrigerated for up to 24 hours. Bring to room temperature for 30 minutes before cooking.

SUGGESTED MENU

Spicy Roasted Drumsticks

Buttered Sweet Potatoes

Steamed Broccoli

Coleslaw

★ Baked Pear Slices

★ *Baked Pear Slices*
Sprinkle pears with granulated sugar, a pinch each cinnamon and ginger; dot with butter and bake, uncovered, in 425° F (220° C) oven for about 30 minutes or until tender.

PREHEAT OVEN TO 425° F (220° C)
FOIL-LINED BAKING SHEET

1/4 cup	Dijon mustard	50 mL
4	cloves garlic, crushed	4
2 tbsp	Worcestershire sauce	25 mL
1 tbsp	vegetable oil	15 mL
2 tsp	Tabasco sauce	10 mL
2 tsp	paprika	10 mL
1/2 tsp	black pepper	2 mL
8	chicken drumsticks, skin scored through (or 3 lbs [1.5 kg] divided wings)	8

1. In a shallow bowl, stir together the mustard, garlic, Worcestershire sauce, oil, Tabasco, paprika and pepper.

2. Dip each drumstick in the mixture and arrange in a single layer on a rack on prepared baking sheet. Cover and let sit for 30 minutes at room temperature.

3. Roast in preheated oven for about 30 minutes or until chicken is no longer pink inside, turning once.

Ground Chicken Pizza

PREHEAT OVEN TO 500° F (260° C)

2 tbsp	olive oil	25 mL
12 oz	lean ground chicken	375 g
8 oz	mushrooms, sliced	250 g
Half	green pepper, in chunks	Half
1	12-inch (30 cm) uncooked pizza crust *or* 1 lb (500 g) pizza dough	1
8 oz	mozzarella or provolone cheese, shredded	250 g
1 tsp	dried Italian herb seasoning	5 mL
1	can (7 1/2 oz [213 mL]) pizza sauce	1

1. In a large skillet, heat half the oil over medium–high heat. Add chicken and cook for 5 minutes, breaking it up with a spoon. Add mushrooms and cook for 5 minutes. Add green pepper and cook for 1 minute.

2. Brush pizza crust with some of the remaining oil; sprinkle with half the cheese. Stir herb seasoning into the sauce; spread over top of the cheese. Arrange chicken mixture on top and sprinkle with remaining cheese. Drizzle with remaining oil. Bake pizza in preheated oven for 12 to 15 minutes or until crust is golden brown.

Herb-Roasted Chicken and Potatoes

Marinating chicken breasts in a lemon juice mixture and roasting at a high temperature produces meat that is juicy on the inside and crisp on the outside — delicious!

SUGGESTED MENU

Herb-Roasted Chicken and Potatoes

♥

★ Maple-Glazed Carrots

♥

Steamed Green Beans

♥

Fresh Fruit

★ **Maple-Glazed Carrots**
In a small amount of boiling, salted water, cook mini peeled carrots or regular sliced carrots until just tender. Drain and return to pan with 2 tbsp (25 mL) each butter and maple syrup. Cook over medium heat, stirring often, for about 3 minutes until glazed and browned.

PREHEAT OVEN TO 425° F (220° C)

4	bone-in chicken breasts	4
2/3 cup	fresh lemon juice	150 mL
2 tbsp	olive oil	25 mL
1/2 tsp	dried rosemary	2 mL
1/2 tsp	dried thyme	2 mL
1/4 tsp	pepper	1 mL
4	potatoes	4
1/2 tsp	salt	2 mL

1. Place chicken in a glass bowl. In a small bowl, combine lemon juice, oil, rosemary, thyme and pepper. Reserve 1/3 cup (75 mL) of the mixture and pour remainder over the chicken; toss to coat well. Cover and let stand at room temperature for 30 minutes.

2. Meanwhile, peel the potatoes and cut into 2-inch (5 cm) cubes; toss with the reserved 1/3 cup (75 mL) marinade.

3. Reserving any marinade from the chicken, place breasts skin-side up in a large shallow roasting pan. Arrange potatoes and their marinade around the edge of the pan. Sprinkle everything with salt and roast in preheated oven for 25 to 30 minutes or until chicken is no longer pink inside. Turn potatoes halfway through cooking time and pour remaining marinade over chicken. Do not overcook.

Sautés and Skillet Suppers

Basque Drumsticks

If you happen to have prosciutto or ham on hand, it adds an extra traditional flavor to this one-dish supper.

MAKE AHEAD

The stew can be entirely made ahead, cooled, covered and refrigerated for up to 1 day. Reheat slowly to serve.

SUGGESTED MENU

Basque Drumsticks

Rice

Green Salad

Fresh Fruit

2 tbsp	olive oil	25 mL
8	drumsticks	8
	Salt and pepper	
2	onions, thickly sliced	2
1	can (28 oz [796 mL]) diced tomatoes	1
2	red or yellow bell peppers, sliced	2
1 cup	coarsely chopped prosciutto or ham (optional)	250 mL
8	cloves garlic, thinly sliced	8
1 tsp	dried thyme	5 mL
1 tsp	paprika	5 mL
1/4 tsp	hot pepper flakes	1 mL
1	orange	1

1. In a deep skillet or shallow saucepan, heat oil. Add chicken and sauté until browned. Season to taste with salt and pepper. Transfer chicken to a plate.

2. Add onions to the skillet and cook for 3 minutes. Stir in tomatoes, peppers, prosciutto, garlic, thyme, paprika and hot pepper flakes. Add back chicken and any juices. Bring to a boil, stirring up any bits from the bottom. Grate zest from orange into stew. Peel orange and coarsely chop fruit; add to stew. Cover and simmer for 20 minutes or until the chicken is no longer pink inside.

Chicken and Pear Sauté

SERVES 4

Sautéed pears are delicious with chicken under a sweet tangy glaze.

SUGGESTED MENU

Chicken and Pear Sauté

❦

Brown Rice

❦

Steamed Asparagus or
Green Beans

❦

Buttered Baby Carrots

❦

Coffee Ice Cream

4	skinless boneless chicken breasts, patted dry	4
	Salt and pepper	
1/2 tsp	dried thyme	2 mL
1/2 tsp	dried sage	2 mL
2 tbsp	butter	25 mL
1 tbsp	vegetable oil	15 mL
2	pears, unpeeled and sliced	2
1	small red onion, chopped	1
1	clove garlic, minced	1
1/4 cup	apple jelly	50 mL
1 tbsp	Dijon mustard	15 mL
	Chopped fresh parsley	

1. Sprinkle chicken with salt and pepper to taste, then with thyme and sage.
2. In a large skillet, melt half the butter with the oil over medium-high heat; cook chicken 5 minutes a side, turning once, until no longer pink inside. Remove to a warm platter to keep warm.
3. Melt remaining butter over medium heat. Add pears, onion and garlic; cook, stirring occasionally for 4 to 5 minutes or until pears are almost tender. Stir in jelly and mustard; cook for 2 minutes. Return chicken to heat through. Sprinkle with parsley to serve.

Crisp Parmesan Chicken

This flavorful chicken has a lovely texture that would go well with orzo and any number of crisply cooked vegetables. However, it might be fun to heat a small jar of meatless spaghetti sauce, boil some pasta and combine the two with a generous sprinkle of Parmesan cheese as an accompaniment for the chicken.

MAKE AHEAD

Recipe can be prepared to the end of step 3, covered and refrigerated for up to 8 hours.

SUGGESTED MENU

Crisp Parmesan Chicken

Spaghetti with Sauce
OR
Buttered Mashed
Potatoes and Steamed
Carrot Slices

Green Salad

Garlic Bread

2	skinless boneless chicken breasts	2
	Salt and pepper	
1/4 cup	all-purpose flour	50 mL
1	egg	1
1/2 cup	freshly grated Parmesan cheese	125 mL
1/4 tsp	dried oregano	1 mL
1/4 tsp	dried basil	1 mL
1 tbsp	olive oil	15 mL

1. Place chicken between 2 pieces of plastic wrap and pound with a mallet or rolling pin to an even thickness of about 1/4 inch (5 mm). Pat dry and sprinkle with salt and pepper.

2. Place flour on waxed paper. In a shallow bowl, beat egg with 1 tbsp (15 mL) cold water. In another shallow bowl, mix cheese with oregano and basil.

3. Dust each breast with flour, dip in egg and coat with cheese. Place on a plate and refrigerate if making ahead.

4. In a large skillet, heat oil over medium-high heat. Add chicken and cook 3 minutes. Using a wide spatula to get all the crust, turn and cook 1 to 2 minutes longer or until no longer pink inside.

Elizabeth Baird's Balsamic-Glazed Chicken Breasts

This was our star chicken dish in a menu Elizabeth and I did for a *Canadian Living* article to show that two people can prepare a pretty impressive dinner party for six in 60 minutes. The chicken itself took little more than 10 minutes with its instant glaze of balsamic vinegar.

SUGGESTED MENU

Antipasto Platter of Prosciutto Curls, Italian Cheese, Olives and Cherry Tomatoes

❧

Balsamic-Glazed Chicken Breasts

❧

★ Gingered Sweet Potatoes

❧

Green Beans

❧

Salad of Mixed Greens

❧

Mocha Sundaes

★ *Gingered Sweet Potatoes*
Add 2 tbsp (25 mL) sour cream and 1/4 tsp (1 mL) each ground ginger, salt and pepper to hot mashed cooked sweet potatoes.

6	skinless boneless chicken breasts	6
1 tsp	dried thyme	5 mL
1/2 tsp	salt	2 mL
1/4 tsp	pepper	1 mL
2 tsp	vegetable oil	10 mL
2 tbsp	balsamic or wine vinegar	25 mL
1 tsp	liquid honey	5 mL
1 tbsp	butter, cut into bits	15 mL

1. Sprinkle both sides of chicken breasts with thyme, salt and pepper. In a large skillet, heat oil over medium-high heat. Add chicken, placing it smooth-side down; cook for 2 minutes or until browned. Turn and brown lightly on underside. Transfer to a plate.

2. Pour 1/3 cup (75 mL) water, balsamic vinegar and honey into the skillet; bring to a boil over high heat, stirring to scrape up any brown bits from the bottom of the pan. Boil for 2 minutes or until slightly syrupy and reduced by half. Add butter; stir until melted.

3. Reduce heat to medium-low. Return chicken, smooth-side down, to pan; cook, turning halfway through, for about 6 minutes or until glazed and no longer pink inside. Serve drizzled with glaze.

Quick Cacciatore

There's lots of old-fashioned flavor in this easy updated version of a popular chicken dish.

MAKE AHEAD

This skillet stew can be completely made ahead, cooled, covered and refrigerated for up to 1 day. Reheat gently to serve.

1 lb	skinless boneless chicken breasts	500 g
	All-purpose flour	
	Salt and pepper	
2 tbsp	olive oil	25 mL
1	onion, chopped	1
1/2 tsp	dried oregano	2 mL
1/4 tsp	hot pepper flakes	1 mL
8 oz	mushrooms, quartered	250 g
2	cloves garlic, minced	2
1	can (19 oz [540 mL]) stewed tomatoes	1
1	small green bell pepper, diced	1
1/4 cup	chopped fresh basil (optional)	50 mL

1. Halve chicken breasts crosswise and place between two pieces of plastic wrap; pound to flatten evenly. Sprinkle with flour, salt and pepper; rub into chicken.
2. In a large skillet heat oil over medium-high heat. Add chicken and brown well on both sides. Remove to a plate.
3. Add onion, oregano and hot pepper flakes to skillet; cook 3 minutes. Add mushrooms and garlic; cook 5 minutes. Stir in tomatoes and green pepper; bring to a boil, scraping up any bits from the bottom. Return chicken and any juices. Season with salt and pepper. Reduce heat, cover and simmer for 15 minutes, stirring occasionally. Sprinkle with basil if using.

SUGGESTED MENU

Quick Cacciatore

Buttered Fettuccine with Parmesan Cheese

Steamed Broccoli

Coffee Ice Cream with Chocolate Sauce

Chicken Breasts with Wild Mushroom Sauce

This absolutely delicious treatment of chicken breasts is true company fare. Use any of the so-called "wild" mushrooms that are readily available in supermarkets these days — portobello, oyster, shiitake, brown or a combination. Even good old regular white ones will be delicious.

SUGGESTED MENU

Chicken Breasts with Wild Mushroom Sauce

★ Creamy Mashed Potatoes

Steamed Green Beans

Baby Carrots

Raspberry Sorbet

★ *Creamy Mashed Potatoes*
Boil 5 quartered peeled potatoes in salted water for 15 to 20 minutes until tender. Drain, mash and beat in 4 oz (125 g) light cream cheese, 1/2 cup (125 mL) light sour cream, and salt and pepper to taste.

4	boneless skinless chicken breasts	4
1/2 tsp	dried tarragon	2 mL
	Salt and pepper	
2 tbsp	all-purpose flour	25 mL
1 tbsp	butter	15 mL
2	cloves garlic, minced	2
8 oz	mushrooms, quartered or sliced	250 g
1 1/2 cups	chicken stock	375 mL
1 tbsp	Dijon mustard	15 mL
1/2 cup	whipping (35%) cream	125 mL
	Chopped parsley	

1. Sprinkle chicken with tarragon and a pinch of salt and pepper. Place flour on a piece of waxed paper and coat each breast with some. In a large skillet, heat butter over medium heat. Add chicken and cook for about 8 minutes a side or until no longer pink inside. Remove to a warm platter and keep warm.

2. Add garlic and mushrooms to skillet; cook, stirring for 3 minutes. Add chicken stock and mustard; increase heat to high and boil for 5 minutes. Stir in cream. Boil for 4 minutes or until thickened. Add salt and pepper to taste. Pour over chicken and garnish with parsley.

Chicken Saltimbocca

SERVES 4

Traditionally made with veal and prosciutto, Saltimbocca is also quick and delicious made with chicken breasts. It's a good, easy company meal.

MAKE AHEAD

Recipe can be prepared to the end of step 1, covered and refrigerated for up to 6 hours.

SUGGESTED MENU

Chicken Saltimbocca

★ Parmesan Mashed
Potatoes
or Pasta Tossed with
Garlic Butter

Sautéed Red Pepper and
Zucchini Strips

Cappuccino Ice Cream
Biscotti

★ *Parmesan Mashed*
Potatoes
Add a good drizzle of olive
oil and freshly grated
Parmesan cheese to hot
mashed potatoes just
before serving.

4	skinless boneless chicken breasts	4
8	fresh sage leaves (optional)	8
4	large thin slices prosciutto	4
	Black pepper	
1/4 cup	all-purpose flour	50 mL
2 tbsp	olive oil (approximate)	25 mL
1/4 cup	Marsala wine *or* port	50 mL
3/4 cup	chicken stock	175 mL
1 tbsp	chopped fresh sage (or 1 tsp [5 mL] dried crumbled sage)	15 mL

1. Place chicken breasts between 2 pieces of plastic wrap and pound to an even 1/4-inch (5 mm) thickness. Place 2 sage leaves (if using) on one side of each breast. Cover with a slice of prosciutto, cutting to fit, and pound lightly to make it adhere. Sprinkle with pepper and dust with flour on both sides.

2. In a very large skillet (or 2 smaller ones), heat oil over medium-high heat. Add chicken and sauté, turning once and adding a bit more oil if necessary, 2 to 3 minutes a side or until no longer pink inside. Remove to a warm platter and keep warm.

3. Add Marsala and bring to a boil, scraping up any brown bits. Add stock. (If using 2 skillets, combine in one.) Boil until slightly thickened. Stir in chopped sage; simmer 1 minute. Drizzle over chicken and serve.

Mediterranean Sautéed Chicken and Vegetables

Although this colorful supper requires two pans, it's a whole meal with some crusty bread.

4	skinless boneless chicken breasts	4
1/2 tsp	dried oregano	2 mL
	Salt and pepper	
4 tbsp	olive oil	50 mL
1	small eggplant, diced	1
1	red bell pepper, cut into strips	1
2	small zucchini, sliced	2
2	cloves garlic, minced	2
1 tsp	dried thyme	5 mL
1/4 tsp	cayenne	1 mL
1	tomato, unpeeled and diced	1
4 oz	goat cheese or feta cheese, crumbled	125 g

1. Sprinkle chicken breasts on both sides with oregano and 1/4 tsp (1 mL) each salt and pepper. In a large skillet, heat half the oil over medium-high heat; brown chicken 2 minutes a side. Reduce heat to medium and cook chicken for about 10 minutes, turning once, until no longer pink inside.

2. Meanwhile, in another large skillet, heat remaining oil over medium heat. Add eggplant, sprinkle with salt and pepper to taste; cook for 5 minutes. Add red pepper and cook for 3 minutes. Add zucchini and garlic; cook for 2 minutes. Stir in thyme, cayenne and tomato. Cover and set aside.

3. Remove cooked chicken to a warm platter and keep warm. Add 2 tbsp (25 mL) water to chicken skillet and bring to a boil, stirring up any brown bits from the bottom. Stir into vegetables and reheat if necessary. Arrange around chicken and sprinkle with cheese to serve.

Chicken Breasts with Rhubarb Sauce

The sweet-and-sour flavor of this rhubarb sauce is wonderful with chicken; so don't think that the rhubarb in your backyard is just for pies.

SUGGESTED MENU

Chicken Breasts with
Rhubarb Sauce

❧

Brown Rice

❧

Baby Carrots

❧

Green Peas

❧

Brownie Sundaes

1 tbsp	olive oil	15 mL
4	skinless boneless chicken breasts	4
	Salt and pepper	
1	small onion, minced	1
3 cups	chopped rhubarb	750 mL
2/3 cup	granulated sugar	150 mL
1/4 cup	fresh lemon juice	50 mL
2 tbsp	Dijon mustard	25 mL
2 tsp	cornstarch	10 mL

1. In a large skillet, heat oil over medium–high heat. Add chicken and cook, turning once and sprinkling with salt and pepper, about 5 minutes or until well browned. Remove to a plate to keep warm.
2. Add onion to skillet; reduce heat to medium and cook for 3 minutes. Stir in rhubarb, sugar, lemon juice and mustard; bring to a boil, stirring to scrape up any brown bits in the bottom of the pan.
3. Return the chicken and any accumulated juices. Spoon some of the sauce over top, cover and simmer 10 to 15 minutes or until no longer pink inside.
4. Dissolve cornstarch in 2 tbsp (25 mL) cold water; stir into sauce and cook, stirring, until thickened.

Anne's Thai Chicken Curry

My daughter, Anne Loxton, often makes this curry as one of her quick suppers after a long day at work. If she doesn't have zucchini and red pepper on hand, she will use whatever is in the house — cut green beans, eggplant slices, frozen green peas. Note her low-fat method of cooking the chicken without oil. If you wish, substitute chopped fresh coriander for the basil.

MAKE AHEAD

The curry can be made completely ahead without the basil, covered, and refrigerated for up to 1 day. Reheat in a skillet over low heat and stir in basil.

SHOPPING TIP

Thai red curry paste usually comes in a small jar, and will keep for months in your refrigerator. You'll find it (and coconut milk) in the specialty or international section of the grocery store. If light coconut milk is not available, use regular coconut milk; just keep in mind that it's about 75% higher in fat.

1 lb	skinless boneless chicken breasts	500 g
1	can (14 oz [398 mL]) light coconut milk	1
1 tbsp	Thai red curry paste	15 mL
1 tsp	cornstarch	5 mL
3	small unpeeled potatoes, diced	3
1	small zucchini, sliced	1
1	red bell pepper, cubed	1
1	can (7 oz [199 mL]) sliced bamboo shoots, rinsed and drained	1
	Salt and pepper	
1/2 cup	slivered fresh basil	125 mL

1. Cut chicken into cubes. In a deep, large skillet, heat 3 tbsp (45 mL) of the coconut milk over medium heat. Add curry paste and cook, stirring, until smooth. Add chicken and cook, stirring often, about 5 minutes or until chicken changes color.

2. In a small bowl, dissolve cornstarch in 1 tbsp (15 mL) of the remaining coconut milk and set aside. Stir remaining milk into pan and bring to a boil.

3. Add potatoes; reduce heat, cover and simmer for 5 minutes, stirring occasionally.

4. Add zucchini, red pepper and bamboo shoots; simmer, covered, for 5 minutes. Stir in cornstarch mixture and cook, stirring, until thickened. Stir in salt and pepper to taste and basil to serve over rice.

SUGGESTED MENU

Anne's Thai Chicken
Curry

Basmati Rice

Steamed Broccoli

Fresh Fruit

Chicken and Sausage Couscous

2 tbsp	olive oil	25 mL
1	onion, coarsely chopped	1
1/2 tsp	paprika	2 mL
1/2 tsp	black pepper	2 mL
1/2 tsp	turmeric	2 mL
1/2 tsp	ground cumin	2 mL
1/4 tsp	cayenne pepper	1 mL
8	chicken wings, tips discarded and wings halved at joint	8
1 cup	chicken stock	250 mL
1 tbsp	tomato paste	15 mL
8 oz	smoked sausage, such as turkey kielbasa, cut into 1/2-inch (1 cm) slices	250 g
8 oz	mini peeled carrots	250 g
1 cup	couscous	250 mL
	Chopped fresh parsley	

1. In a shallow medium saucepan, heat oil over medium heat. Add onion and cook for 2 minutes. Stir in paprika, pepper, turmeric, cumin and cayenne; cook for 1 minute. Add wings and toss to coat. Stir in stock, tomato paste, sausage and carrots; bring to a boil, reduce heat, cover and simmer for 15 to 20 minutes or until vegetables are tender and chicken is no longer pink inside.

2. Meanwhile, in a saucepan with a lid, bring 1 1/2 cups (375 mL) water to a boil. Add couscous and 1/2 tsp (2 mL) salt. (Or follow couscous package directions.) Remove from heat. Let stand, covered, for 5 minutes or until couscous is tender and water is absorbed; fluff with a fork.

3. Spoon couscous onto a large heated platter. Make a well in the center and spoon in chicken mixture. Sprinkle generously with parsley.

SUGGESTED MENU

Chicken and Sausage
Couscous

❦

Warm Pita Bread

❦

Green Salad

❦

★ Honey-Poached
Pears

★ *Honey-Poached Pears*
While the couscous cooks, place 4 peeled pears upright in a microwave-proof casserole. Drizzle with 2 tbsp (25 mL) each liquid honey and fresh lemon juice. Cover and cook on High for 5 minutes.

Chicken Braised with Artichoke Hearts and Sun-Dried Tomatoes

2	skinless boneless chicken breasts	2
	Black pepper	
2 tbsp	all-purpose flour	25 mL
1 tbsp	olive oil	15 mL
1	small onion, chopped	1
2	cloves garlic, minced	2
1/4 cup	white wine or vermouth *or* additional chicken stock	50 mL
3/4 cup	chicken stock	175 mL
1	can (14 oz [398 mL]) artichoke hearts, rinsed, drained and quartered	1
1/4 cup	slivered dry-packed sun-dried tomatoes	50 mL
1 tbsp	chopped fresh basil (or 1 tsp [5 mL] dried)	15 mL
1 tbsp	chopped fresh oregano (or 1 tsp [5 mL] dried)	15 mL
1/2 tsp	granulated sugar	2 mL

1. Dry chicken well, sprinkle with pepper and dredge in flour.
2. In a large skillet, heat oil over medium-high heat. Add chicken and brown on both sides. Remove to a plate.
3. Add onion and garlic to the pan; cook over medium heat for 3 minutes.
4. Stir in wine and bring to a boil, scraping up any bits sticking to the bottom of the pan. Stir in stock, artichoke hearts, tomatoes, basil, oregano and sugar. Bring to a boil. Return chicken, reduce heat, cover and simmer for 15 to 20 minutes or until chicken is no longer pink inside.

Lemon-Parsley Chicken

Fresh lemon juice is always a happy companion for chicken — as it is here in this very simple dish.

SUGGESTED MENU

Lemon-Parsley Chicken

↓

Mashed Potatoes

↓

★ Maple-Glazed Carrots

↓

Green Peas

↓

Fresh Fruit Salad

★ **Maple-Glazed Carrots**
Boil baby carrots in salted water until almost tender; drain and add 2 tbsp (25 mL) butter, 1/4 cup (50 mL) maple syrup, and salt and pepper to taste. Cook over medium heat for 3 or 4 minutes or until carrots are tender and glazed.

4	skinless boneless chicken breasts	4
1/4 cup	all-purpose flour	50 mL
1/2 tsp	salt	2 mL
1/2 tsp	pepper	2 mL
1/2 tsp	grated lemon zest	2 mL
1 tbsp	butter	15 mL
1 tbsp	olive oil	15 mL
1/2 cup	chicken stock	125 mL
2 tbsp	fresh lemon juice	25 mL
1	clove garlic, minced	1
2 tbsp	chopped fresh parsley	25 mL

1. Place chicken breasts between 2 pieces of plastic wrap and pound with a mallet or rolling pin to flatten evenly to 1/4 inch (5 mm).

2. In a shallow bowl, stir together flour, salt, pepper and lemon zest; coat both sides of breasts with mixture.

3. In a large skillet, melt butter with oil over medium-high heat. Add chicken and cook about 4 minutes a side, turning once, until golden brown and no longer pink inside. Remove to a warm platter and keep warm.

4. Add chicken stock, lemon juice and garlic to the skillet; bring to a boil and cook, stirring, for 4 to 5 minutes or until thickened. Remove from heat and stir in parsley. Pour over chicken.

Almond Chicken with Peaches and Roquefort

If peaches are not in season, substitute two small pears, cored and sliced for this special main course.

MAKE AHEAD

The chicken can be coated with almonds, put on a plate, covered and refrigerated for up to 4 hours. Bring to room temperature for 30 minutes before cooking.

SUGGESTED MENU

Almond Chicken with Peaches and Roquefort

★ Lemon Couscous

Green Beans

Store-bought Pastries

★ *Lemon Couscous*
Add 1/2 tsp (2 mL) grated lemon zest and 1 tbsp (15 mL) fresh lemon juice to warm couscous.

2	skinless boneless chicken breasts	2
1/4 cup	all-purpose flour	50 mL
	Salt and pepper	
1	egg, lightly beaten	1
3/4 cup	sliced almonds	175 mL
2 tbsp	vegetable oil	25 mL
2	unpeeled peaches, sliced	2
1/4 cup	dry white wine *or* chicken stock	50 mL
1/4 cup	whipping (35%) cream	50 mL
2 tbsp	crumbled Roquefort or Gorgonzola cheese	25 mL

1. Place chicken breasts between 2 pieces of plastic wrap and pound to an even thickness of about 1/4 inch (5 mm). Dredge in flour mixed with 1/4 tsp (1 mL) each salt and pepper. Dip each breast in egg and coat with almonds.

2. In a large skillet, heat half the oil over medium heat. Add chicken and cook about 5 minutes a side, turning once, until golden and no longer pink inside. Remove to a warm platter and keep warm.

3. Add remaining oil to pan and heat over medium heat. Add peaches and cook 1 minute. Stir in wine and bring to a boil; cook 3 minutes to reduce. Stir in cream, cheese, and salt and pepper to taste. Cook, stirring, until thickened. Spoon sauce around the chicken and serve.

Southwestern Chicken and Potato Fry

SERVES 4

This one-dish skillet supper makes use of cooked potatoes left from the previous night's dinner. I particularly like it with little boiled new potatoes, preferably red ones.

SUGGESTED MENU

Southwestern Chicken and Potato Fry

Green Salad

Crusty Brown Rolls and Butter

Orange Sorbet with Ginger Cookies

4	cooked unpeeled medium potatoes (or 12 tiny new potatoes)	4
2 tbsp	olive or vegetable oil	25 mL
1 lb	skinless boneless chicken breasts or thighs, cut into 3/4-inch (2 cm) cubes	500 g
	Salt and pepper	
2	green onions, sliced	2
1 cup	bottled tomato salsa	250 mL
1	can (12 oz [341 mL]) corn kernels, drained	1
2 tbsp	chopped fresh coriander or parsley	25 mL

1. Cut potatoes into 3/4-inch (2 cm) cubes. Set aside.

2. In a large skillet, heat half the oil over medium heat. Add chicken and cook, stirring, for about 5 minutes or until browned and no longer pink inside. Remove chicken with a slotted spoon to a plate and keep warm.

3. Heat remaining oil and add potatoes; sprinkle with salt and pepper and cook for about 8 minutes or until browned, stirring often. Add green onions, cooked chicken, salsa and corn; cook for about 5 minutes to heat through, stirring often. Stir in coriander to serve.

Maple Chicken Sautéed with Dried Fruit

Fruit goes so well with chicken, and a touch of maple syrup gilds the lily in this simple skillet supper dish. Use a mix of dried apples, pears, apricots, prunes or whatever you happen to have on hand.

SUGGESTED MENU

Maple Chicken Sautéed
with Dried Fruit

❧

Rice

❧

Winter Squash Slices

❧

Green Salad

❧

Cake and Ice Cream

6 oz	mixed dried fruits (about 1 1/2 cups [375 mL])	175 g
4	skinless boneless chicken breasts	4
	Salt and pepper	
1/2 tsp	dried sage	2 mL
1/2 tsp	dried thyme	2 mL
1 tbsp	butter	15 mL
1/3 cup	chopped shallots or mild onions	75 mL
3 tbsp	maple syrup	45 mL

1. Pour 1 1/2 cups (375 mL) boiling water over fruit; allow to steep while preparing remaining ingredients.

2. Place chicken breasts between two pieces of plastic wrap and pound slightly. Season with 1/2 tsp (2 mL) each salt and pepper, sage and thyme.

3. In a large skillet, melt butter over medium heat. Add chicken and cook 2 minutes a side or until browned. Add shallots; cook 30 seconds. Add fruit and liquid; cook for 5 minutes, uncovered, until chicken is no longer pink inside. Stir in maple syrup and cook 1 minute.

4. Remove chicken to a warm platter and keep warm. Boil sauce for about 3 minutes until syrupy. Spoon sauce over chicken and serve.

Quick Coq Au Vin

You'll be surprised at how much this quick and easy version tastes like the long-cooking dinner party favorite.

SHOPPING TIP

Use frozen peeled pearl onions if you can find them. If not, to speed peeling, immerse in boiling water for 2 minutes, refresh in cold water; slip off skins.

SUGGESTED MENU

Quick Coq au Vin

❧

Creamy Mashed
Potatoes

❧

★ Butter-Sautéed
Mushrooms

❧

Green Salad

❧

Apple Tart

★ *Butter-Sautéed*
Mushrooms
In a large skillet, cook
small whole mushrooms in
butter over medium-high
heat for 7 minutes or until
browned and liquid has
evaporated. Sprinkle with
salt and pepper to serve.

4	slices bacon	4
4	skinless boneless chicken breasts	4
	Salt and pepper	
	All-purpose flour	
1 1/2 cups	peeled pearl onions	375 mL
1 1/4 cups	dry red wine	300 mL
3/4 cup	chicken stock	175 mL
1	clove garlic, minced	1
1 tsp	dried thyme	5 mL
	Chopped fresh parsley	

1. In a large heavy skillet, cook bacon until crisp. Transfer to paper towels to drain off extra fat. Crumble when cool. Pour off all but 2 tbsp (25 mL) drippings from the skillet.

2. Sprinkle chicken with salt and pepper; coat with flour. Add to skillet and cook over medium heat for 4 minutes. Turn, add onions and cook another 4 minutes. Transfer chicken to a plate.

3. Increase heat to high; stir in wine, stock, garlic and thyme. Bring to a boil, scraping up any brown bits. Reduce heat to medium-low and simmer, uncovered, for 12 minutes. Return chicken and any juices to skillet. Simmer for 10 to 12 minutes or until chicken is cooked through, turning once.

4. Transfer chicken to heated plates. Spoon sauce over top; garnish with bacon and chopped parsley.

Pecan Chicken Cutlets

These moist chicken breasts, with their decadent coating, make excellent company fare.

The chicken can be coated, covered and refrigerated (end of step 2) for up to 4 hours before cooking.

★ **Tomato Salad**
Drizzle tomato wedges with a mustard vinaigrette of 1/3 cup (75 mL) olive oil, 1 tbsp (15 mL) white wine vinegar, 1 tsp (5 mL) Dijon mustard, and salt and pepper to taste. Sprinkle with slivered fresh basil leaves or chopped fresh parsley.

★ **Nutmeg-Scented Spinach**
Add a pinch of freshly grated nutmeg to hot cooked spinach.

★ **Plum Tart**
Roll out thawed puff pastry to make a 12-inch (30 cm) square and arrange prune plum quarters on top. Sprinkle with sugar and lemon juice; bake in 450° F (230° C) oven for about 20 minutes.

4	skinless boneless chicken breasts	4
1 1/4 cups	pecan halves or pieces	300 mL
1/4 cup	all-purpose flour	50 mL
1/3 cup	buttermilk	75 mL
2 tbsp	olive oil (approximate)	25 mL
2 tbsp	raspberry vinegar	25 mL

1. Place chicken between two pieces of plastic wrap and pound to an even 1/4-inch (5 mm) thickness.

2. Place pecans and flour in a food processor and process until nuts are finely chopped. Spread mixture out slightly on a piece of waxed paper. Pour buttermilk into a shallow bowl. Dip each chicken breast in the buttermilk; then in the pecan mixture to coat well.

3. Heat oil over medium heat. Cook coated breasts 10 to 12 minutes, turning once and adding more oil if necessary, until no longer pink inside. Remove to a heated platter and keep warm.

4. Add 1/4 cup (50 mL) water and vinegar to the pan and bring to a boil, stirring up any brown bits from the bottom. Drizzle mixture over cutlets to serve.

SUGGESTED MENU

Pecan Chicken Cutlets

★ Tomato Salad

★ Nutmeg-Scented Spinach
or Steamed Green Beans

Crusty Bread

★ Plum Tart

Chicken Frittata

My good friend and able assistant, Sharon Boyd, often makes a frittata for her family using whatever is at hand in her refrigerator. Feel free to use whatever you want in this easy supper dish. Add a small sliced zucchini or some chopped broccoli with the pepper; or substitute corn for the peas; add some sliced cooked potatoes with the chicken. It's also a good way to use up ends of cheese; Fontina, Cheddar or provolone are all good melting cheeses.

SUGGESTED MENU

Chicken Frittata

Whole-grain Bread

Green Salad

Fresh Fruit

PREHEAT BROILER

6	eggs	6
1/2 tsp	salt	2 mL
1/4 tsp	pepper	1 mL
1/4 tsp	dried thyme	1 mL
1/4 tsp	oregano	1 mL
1 tbsp	butter	15 mL
1 tbsp	vegetable oil	15 mL
1	onion, chopped	1
1	small red bell pepper, diced	1
1 cup	diced cooked chicken	250 mL
1 cup	frozen peas	250 mL
1 1/2 cups	shredded Swiss cheese	375 mL

1. In a bowl whisk together eggs, salt, pepper, thyme and oregano. Set aside.

2. In a large ovenproof skillet, melt butter with oil over medium heat. Add onion and red pepper; cook for about 5 minutes until softened. Stir in chicken and peas; spread out in pan. Pour egg mixture on top. Cook for 7 to 10 minutes, tilting pan occasionally and pulling mixture from sides with a spatula, until eggs start to set around the edge but center still jiggles slightly.

3. Sprinkle with cheese. Place skillet about 5 inches (12.5 cm) from heat and broil 3 minutes or until golden brown and set. Cut in wedges to serve.

Hoisin Orange Chicken

I love the flavor of hoisin and orange together in this fast, fresh sauté.

VARIATION

You can use this sauce as a marinade to make flavorful grilled chicken. Decrease the orange juice by half and don't add the salt and pepper until just before cooking. You can marinate the chicken up to 8 hours in the refrigerator, bringing to room temperature for 30 minutes before cooking. When you remove the chicken to the barbecue, pour the marinade into a small saucepan and boil for 1 minute; stir in 1 tbsp (15 mL) orange marmalade and use as a glaze.

4	skinless boneless chicken breasts	4
	Salt and pepper	
1 tbsp	vegetable oil	15 mL
2	cloves garlic, minced	2
1 tsp	grated orange zest	5 mL
1/2 cup	fresh orange juice	125 mL
1/4 cup	hoisin sauce	50 mL
1 tbsp	minced ginger root	15 mL
Pinch	hot pepper flakes	Pinch

1. Sprinkle chicken breasts lightly with salt and pepper. In a large skillet, heat oil over medium-high heat. Add chicken and cook for about 5 minutes a side or until golden outside and no longer pink inside. Transfer to a warm plate and keep warm.

2. Add garlic to skillet; cook for 1 minute. In a small bowl, combine orange zest, orange juice, hoisin sauce, ginger and hot pepper flakes. Add to skillet and bring to a boil; cook, stirring, for 3 minutes or until thickened slightly.

3. Return chicken to the skillet, turning to coat; heat through. Serve with sauce spooned over top.

SUGGESTED MENU

Hoisin Orange Chicken

Chinese Noodles

Steamed Asparagus

Strawberries with Brown Sugar and Sour Cream

Chicken Scaloppine

This really simple treatment of chicken breasts results in a delightfully tender and delicious treat you'll want to make time after time. If you wish, you can name it "schnitzel" and accompany it with applesauce and coleslaw, the way the pubs serve pork schnitzel in the region of Waterloo, Ontario.

SUGGESTED MENU

Chicken Scaloppine

❧

★ Oven-Roasted Vegetables

❧

Crusty Italian Bread

❧

Green Salad

❧

Lemon Ice Cream
Espresso

★ *Oven-Roasted Vegetables*
In a large shallow pan, toss sliced bell pepper, quartered mushrooms and sliced zucchini with olive oil; spread out and roast in 450° F (230° C) oven for about 20 to 25 minutes or until vegetables are softened, stirring once or twice. Season with salt and pepper, and herbs such as basil and rosemary.

4	skinless boneless chicken breasts	4
	Salt and pepper	
2	eggs	2
1 1/2 cups	dry bread crumbs	375 mL
2 tbsp	butter	25 mL
	Minced parsley (optional)	
	Lemon wedges	

1. Slice each chicken breast in half horizontally to make 8 thin pieces. Place between 2 pieces of plastic wrap and pound as thin as possible. Sprinkle with salt and pepper.

2. In a flat baking dish or bowl, beat eggs with 1/4 cup (50 mL) water to combine. Spread crumbs out in a pie plate or on waxed paper. Dip each breast in the egg, then coat with bread crumbs all over. Lay in a single layer on a cookie sheet to dry for 10 minutes.

3. In each of 2 large skillets over medium-high heat, melt half the butter. Add chicken breasts and cook for 2 to 3 minutes a side, turning once, until golden brown. Sprinkle with parsley, if using, and serve immediately with lemon wedges.

Chicken Shepherd's Pie

Cook extra potatoes the night before you prepare this lean, delicious version of an old favorite. Or boil peeled, quartered potatoes while the chicken cooks. And if you have leftover vegetables, you can also chop them to use instead of the frozen variety.

MAKE AHEAD

Both the chicken mixture and potato topping can be made ahead, covered and refrigerated up to 1 day. Bring chicken to a simmer before proceeding. Or complete the whole pie, cover and refrigerate. Warm gently to a simmer, then broil.

SUGGESTED MENU

Chicken Shepherd's Pie

Chili Sauce

Coleslaw

Applesauce and Cookies

1 tsp	vegetable oil	5 mL
1	onion, chopped	1
1	clove garlic, chopped	1
1 lb	ground chicken	500 g
1 tbsp	all-purpose flour	15 mL
1 cup	chicken stock	250 mL
2 cups	frozen mixed vegetables	500 mL
1 tbsp	ketchup	15 mL
1 tbsp	Worcestershire sauce	15 mL
1/2 tsp	dried sage	2 mL
1/2 tsp	dried thyme	2 mL
	Salt and pepper	
4 oz	light cream cheese, softened	125 g
1	egg	1
4 cups	mashed potatoes	1 L

1. In a deep 10-inch (25 cm) ovenproof skillet, heat oil over medium heat. Add onion and garlic; cook for 3 minutes or until soft. Add chicken; cook, breaking up with the back of a spoon, for 5 to 7 minutes or until no longer pink. Sprinkle with flour; cook, stirring, for 1 minute. Gradually stir in stock; raise heat and cook, stirring, until thickened.

2. Stir in vegetables, ketchup, Worcestershire sauce, sage and thyme; bring to a boil. Reduce heat and simmer uncovered for 5 minutes. Season with salt and pepper to taste.

Recipe continues...

ALMOND CHICKEN WITH PEACHES AND ROQUEFORT (PAGE 120) ➤
OVERLEAF: GROUND CHICKEN PIZZA (PAGE 102)

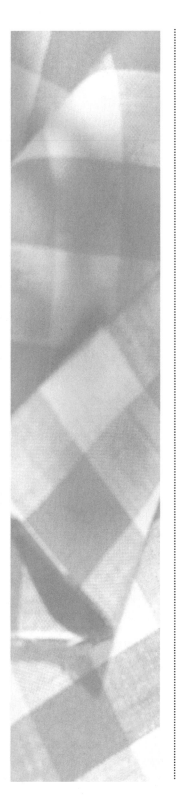

3. Meanwhile, beat cheese and egg into potatoes. Season with salt and pepper to taste. Spoon over chicken mixture. Place pan (covering handle with foil if not ovenproof) in the bottom third of the oven and broil for 7 to 8 minutes or until potatoes are heated through and golden brown.

◄ CHICKEN CHILI MACARONI (PAGE 147)

Skillet Chicken Stroganoff

Anyone who likes mushrooms with chicken in a creamy sauce will love this quick and easy skillet supper. Serve on top of hot buttered egg noodles.

SHOPPING TIPS

To save time, look for chicken already cut into stir-fry strips. Also look for prepackaged sliced mushrooms.

1 tbsp	butter	15 mL
1 tbsp	vegetable oil	15 mL
1 lb	skinless boneless chicken breasts or thighs, cut into thin strips	500 g
	Salt and pepper	
2 cups	tiny whole mushrooms or sliced large mushrooms	500 mL
1	red bell pepper, cut into strips	1
2	cloves garlic, minced	2
4 tsp	Dijon mustard	20 mL
1 tbsp	Worcestershire sauce	15 mL
2/3 cup	light sour cream	150 mL
	Chopped parsley (optional)	

1. In a large skillet, melt butter with oil over medium-high heat. Add chicken and cook, stirring often, for 5 minutes or until it changes color. Sprinkle with salt and pepper.

2. Add mushrooms, red pepper and garlic; cook, stirring often, for 4 minutes. Reduce heat to low; stir in mustard, Worcestershire sauce and sour cream. Taste and adjust seasoning. Heat through but do not boil. Sprinkle with parsley if desired.

SUGGESTED MENU

Skillet Chicken
Stroganoff

Buttered Egg Noodles

Baby Carrots

Green Peas
or Green Salad

Baked Apples

Chicken Thighs with Curried Tomato Sauce

1 tbsp	vegetable oil	15 mL
1	onion, chopped	1
2 tbsp	all-purpose flour	25 mL
2 tbsp	curry powder	25 mL
1	can (19 oz [540 mL]) tomatoes	1
1/2 cup	seedless raisins	125 mL
2	cloves garlic, minced	2
1 tbsp	fresh lemon juice	15 mL
8	chicken thighs	8
2 tbsp	chopped fresh parsley	25 mL

1. In a large skillet, heat oil over medium-low heat. Add onion and cook for 3 minutes. Add flour and curry powder; cook, stirring, for 2 minutes. Add tomatoes, raisins, garlic and lemon juice; bring to a boil, stirring.

2. Add thighs and cook, covered, over medium heat, for about 25 minutes, turning once, until chicken is no longer pink inside. Uncover, stir in parsley and cook a minute or two longer to thicken if desired.

Braised Chicken with New Potatoes and Peas

SERVES 4

This easy skillet stew highlights new little red potatoes. If these are not in season, you can use chunks of bigger storage potatoes.

MAKE AHEAD

The skillet stew can be completely made ahead, cooled, covered and refrigerated for up to 1 day. Reheat gently, stirring often, to serve.

SUGGESTED MENU

Braised Chicken with
New Potatoes and Peas

☙

Green Salad

☙

Stewed Rhubarb

4	slices side bacon, diced	4
4	skinless boneless chicken breasts	4
1	onion, chopped	1
1	green pepper, chopped	1
1	clove garlic, minced	1
1 tbsp	sweet paprika	15 mL
1 1/2 cups	chicken stock	375 mL
8	small new red potatoes, halved	8
1 cup	frozen peas	250 mL
1/2 cup	light sour cream	125 mL
2 tsp	all-purpose flour	10 mL
	Salt and pepper	

1. In a large skillet over medium heat, cook bacon until almost crisp. Remove with a slotted spoon and set aside.

2. Pour off all but 2 tbsp (25 mL) drippings. Brown chicken in drippings over medium-high heat. Remove to a plate.

3. Add onion to pan and cook 5 minutes. Stir in green pepper, garlic and reserved bacon; cook 30 seconds. Stir in paprika to coat vegetables well. Stir in stock, return chicken and arrange potatoes around it.

4. Bring to a simmer, cover and cook over medium-low heat for 10 to 15 minutes or until chicken is no longer pink inside and potatoes are tender. Remove chicken and potatoes to a heated platter.

5. Add peas to skillet. Boil to reduce sauce if necessary, then reduce heat to low. Stir sour cream and flour together; add to sauce and cook, stirring, to heat through, but do not boil. Season with salt and pepper and pour over chicken.

Braised Chicken with Eggplant and Chickpeas

SERVES 4

If you wish, substitute 4 skinless boneless chicken breasts for the drumsticks in this hearty one-dish supper. Small eggplants don't require any salting.

SUGGESTED MENU

Braised Chicken with
Eggplant and
Chickpeas

❦

Rice

❦

Green Beans

❦

Orange Wedges

2	small eggplants	2
3 tbsp	olive oil (approximate)	45 mL
8	chicken drumsticks	8
2	onions, sliced	2
2	cloves garlic, minced	2
1/2 tsp	ground cumin	2 mL
1/2 tsp	allspice	2 mL
1	can (28 oz [796 mL]) tomatoes	1
1	can (19 oz [540 mL]) chickpeas, rinsed and drained	1
3 tbsp	fresh lemon juice	45 mL
	Salt and pepper	
2 tbsp	chopped fresh parsley	25 mL

1. Trim eggplants, cut in half lengthwise and slice across. In a very large deep skillet, heat 2 tbsp (25 mL) oil over medium-high heat. Add eggplant and cook, stirring often, until golden brown. Remove with a slotted spoon to drain on paper towels.

2. Add 1 tbsp (15 mL) oil to the pan and brown chicken on all sides; push to one side of pan.

3. Add onions and cook 3 minutes, adding more oil if necessary. Stir in garlic, cumin and allspice, arranging chicken pieces evenly around pan. Add tomatoes, chickpeas, lemon juice, and 1/4 tsp (1 mL) each salt and pepper. Bring to a boil; reduce heat, cover and simmer for 15 minutes. Add browned eggplant and simmer about 10 minutes longer or until chicken is no longer pink inside. Taste and adjust seasoning. Sprinkle with parsley to serve.

Monda Rosenberg's Lime-Ginger Chicken

SERVES 4

Monda Rosenberg, the food editor of *Chatelaine* (and my longtime good friend), has a knack for putting a few ingredients together to get good taste without a lot of fuss — as in this great recipe from her bestselling book, *Quickies*, published McClelland & Stewart Inc.

2 tbsp	butter	25 mL
4	skinless boneless chicken breasts	4
2 tbsp	finely chopped ginger in syrup, drained	25 mL
1 tbsp	fresh lime juice	15 mL
Pinch	white pepper	Pinch

1. In a large skillet, melt butter over medium heat. Add chicken breasts and cook 3 minutes a side.
2. Add ginger, lime juice and white pepper; cook over low heat 4 minutes a side.

SUGGESTED MENU

Lime-Ginger Chicken

❧

Sweet Potato Slices

❧

★ Garlic Green Beans

❧

Cherry Tomatoes

❧

Baked Apples

★ *Garlic Green Beans*
Cook green beans, uncovered, in a large amount of salted boiling water for about 4 minutes or just until tender-crisp; drain well. Sauté minced garlic in olive oil for 1 minute; add beans and cook 1 minute.

Quick Chicken Chili

A short cooking time gives freshness and crunch to the vegetables in this easy, light version of an old favorite.

MAKE AHEAD

The chili can be made up to 2 days ahead and reheated gently (adding remaining green pepper just before serving).

VARIATION

Fill taco shells or warm flour tortillas with hot chili and top with shredded lettuce, sour cream, shredded Cheddar cheese and bottled salsa.

SUGGESTED MENU

Quick Chicken Chili

Crusty Rolls

Green Salad

Fresh Fruit

1 tbsp	vegetable oil	15 mL
1	onion, chopped	1
2	cloves garlic, crushed	2
1	green pepper, chopped	1
2 tbsp	chili powder	25 mL
1 tsp	ground cumin	5 mL
1 tsp	dried oregano	5 mL
Pinch	hot pepper flakes	Pinch
1 lb	lean ground chicken	500 g
1	can (28 oz [796 mL]) tomatoes, preferably diced	1
1	can (19 oz [540 mL]) white kidney beans, rinsed and drained	1
1	stalk celery, sliced	1

1. In a large saucepan, heat oil over medium heat. Add onion, garlic and half the green pepper; cook for 3 minutes. Add chili powder, cumin, oregano and hot pepper flakes; cook, stirring, for 2 minutes or until fragrant. Add chicken, raise heat and cook, breaking up with a spoon, for 5 minutes until chicken changes color.

2. Stir in tomatoes, beans and celery. Cook, covered, for 15 minutes, stirring occasionally. Mash some of the beans against the side of the pan to thicken chili slightly. Stir in remaining green pepper.

Pasta and Rice

Chicken and Broccoli Pasta with Pesto

This colorful main dish takes only minutes to make.

SHOPPING TIPS

To save time, buy pre-cut broccoli florets and chicken already cut in strips.

12 oz	penne	375 g
2 tbsp	olive oil	25 mL
1 lb	boneless, skinless chicken breasts cut into 1/2-inch (1 cm) strips	500 g
1	red bell pepper, cut into strips	1
8 oz	small broccoli florets (4 cups [1 L])	250 g
1	container (6.5 oz [185 g]) pesto (about 3/4 cup [175 mL])	1
1/3 cup	freshly grated Parmesan cheese	75 mL
	Additional freshly grated Parmesan	

1. In a large pot of boiling salted water, cook the penne for 8 to 10 minutes or until tender but firm.

2. Meanwhile, in a large skillet, heat oil over medium-high heat. Add chicken and red pepper; cook for 3 to 5 minutes, stirring often, or until the chicken is cooked through. Set aside.

3. Place the broccoli in a colander and drain the pasta over it. Place back in the pot. Stir in the pesto, the contents of the skillet and the cheese. Serve immediately with additional cheese for sprinkling at the table.

★ Spinach and Mushroom Salad
For a homemade dressing to top fresh spinach and sliced mushrooms, whisk together 1/3 cup (75 mL) light sour cream, 2 tbsp (25 mL) each milk and light mayonnaise, 2 tsp (10 mL) each granulated sugar and cider vinegar, a minced garlic clove, and salt and pepper to taste.

★ Cinnamon Bananas with Honey Yogurt
Cut peeled bananas lengthwise, sprinkle with brown sugar, dots of butter and cinnamon; broil close to the element for 3 to 5 minutes and serve with plain yogurt sweetened with honey.

SUGGESTED MENU

Chicken & Broccoli Pasta with Pesto

Whole Wheat Rolls

★ Spinach and Mushroom Salad

★ Cinnamon Bananas with Honey Yogurt

Creamy Bow-Ties with Chicken and Asparagus

If asparagus is not in season, substitute a package of frozen asparagus in this quick pasta supper.

SHOPPING TIP

For speedier preparation, look for already cut stir-fry chicken strips in the supermarket.

SUGGESTED MENU

Creamy Bow-ties with Chicken and Asparagus

Brown Rolls

Green Salad

Cherry Tomatoes

🖝

Stewed Rhubarb

12 oz	bow-tie pasta (farfalle)	375 g
8 oz	asparagus cut into 1 1/2-inch (3 cm) pieces	250 g
2 tbsp	butter	25 mL
1 tbsp	olive oil	15 mL
12 oz	skinless boneless chicken breasts or thighs, cut into 1/2-inch (1 cm) strips	375 g
4 oz	mushrooms, quartered	125 g
2	cloves garlic, minced	2
1 tsp	dried Italian herb seasoning	5 mL
8 oz	spreadable light cream cheese	250 g
1/3 to 2/3 cup	milk	75 to 150 mL

Salt and pepper

1. In a large pot of boiling salted water, cook the pasta for 4 minutes. Add asparagus and cook for 4 to 6 minutes or until the pasta is tender but firm and the asparagus is tender. Drain well and return to the pot.

2. Meanwhile, in a large skillet, melt butter with oil over medium-high heat. Add chicken and cook, stirring often, for 5 minutes or until it changes color. Add mushrooms and garlic; cook for 7 minutes or until chicken and mushrooms are browned. Stir in seasoning. Add to pasta with cheese. Return pot to medium heat. Stir in enough milk to make a creamy sauce; cook until heated through. Season to taste with salt and pepper.

If you don't have fresh sage for this delicious use of cooked chicken, choose another favorite fresh herb like basil or parsley.

SHOPPING TIP

Roasted peppers are available in jars in every supermarket. Drain before using.

SUGGESTED MENU

Sage-Buttered Tortellini with Chicken and Roasted Peppers

❧

Green Salad

❧

Crusty Bread

❧

Fresh Fruit

Sage-Buttered Tortellini with Chicken and Roasted Peppers

12 oz	fresh or frozen cheese tortellini or agnolotti	375 g
1 1/2 cups	frozen green peas	375 mL
2 tbsp	olive oil	25 mL
1 cup	roasted red pepper strips	250 mL
2 tbsp	butter	25 mL
2 tbsp	chopped fresh sage	25 mL
2 cups	cooked chicken strips	500 mL
	Salt and pepper	

1. In a large pot of boiling salted water, cook pasta according to the package directions, adding peas during the last minute of cooking. Drain well. Transfer to a large bowl and stir in olive oil and red peppers. Keep warm.

2. In the same pot, melt butter over medium heat. Add sage and cook, stirring, for 1 minute. Stir in the chicken and salt and pepper to taste; heat through. Stir into the tortellini.

Chicken and Pasta with Red Pepper Sauce

Like a grown-up version of a boxed pasta dinner, this easy, monochromatic pasta dish gets a hit of flavor from bottled roasted red peppers. Serve with extra cheese if desired.

MAKE AHEAD

The sauce can be made up to 8 hours ahead, covered and refrigerated. Bring to room temperature to use.

SHOPPING TIP

For convenience, look for chicken already cut into strips or tenderloins. Roasted red peppers are usually found in the condiment-pickle section of the supermarket.

12 oz	fusilli	375 g
2 tbsp	olive oil	25 mL
12 oz	skinless boneless chicken breasts, cut into 1/2-inch (1 cm) strips	375 g
2	cloves garlic, chopped	2
1/4 tsp	hot pepper flakes	1 mL
1 cup	well drained bottled roasted red peppers (loosely packed)	250 mL
1/2 cup	light mayonnaise	125 mL
1 tbsp	fresh lemon juice	15 mL
	Salt and pepper	
1/2 cup	freshly grated Parmesan cheese	125 mL

1. In a large pot of boiling salted water, cook the fusilli for 8 to 10 minutes or until tender but firm.

2. Meanwhile, in a large skillet, heat the oil over medium-high heat. Add chicken, garlic and hot pepper flakes; cook, stirring often, for 4 to 5 minutes, or until the chicken has changed color.

3. While the chicken cooks, place red peppers, mayonnaise and lemon juice in a blender; purée until smooth. Season to taste with salt and pepper. Stir into the cooked chicken over low heat.

4. Drain pasta and toss with chicken mixture and cheese. Adjust seasoning to taste.

★ *Sage Leaf Focaccia*
Soak 24 small fresh or dried sage leaves in 2 tbsp (25 mL) olive oil. Sprinkle onto a prepared pizza crust or flatbread; sprinkle with salt and pepper and freshly grated Parmesan cheese. Bake in 425° F (220° C) oven for 20 minutes or until golden.

SUGGESTED MENU

Chicken and Pasta with Red Pepper Sauce

Green Salad

★ Sage Leaf Focaccia or Crusty Rolls

Fresh Fruit

Penne with Herbed Chicken Sauce

Fresh herbs are highlighted in this easy pasta dish, but if they are not available, it is still delicious with dried. You will probably want to serve it with freshly grated Parmesan cheese for spooning on top.

MAKE AHEAD

The chicken sauce can be completely prepared to the end of step 2, cooled, covered and refrigerated for up to 1 day or frozen for up to 3 months. (If frozen, thaw in the refrigerator overnight.) Reheat gently, stirring often, to serve.

SUGGESTED MENU

Penne with Herbed
Chicken Sauce

Crusty Bread

Green Salad

Fresh Fruit

2 tbsp	olive oil	25 mL
4	cloves garlic, minced	4
1 lb	ground chicken	500 g
1	can (28 oz [796 mL]) crushed tomatoes	1
1/2 cup	dry red wine	125 mL
1/2 cup	chopped fresh parsley	125 mL
1/2 cup	chopped fresh basil (or 4 tsp [20 mL] dried)	125 mL
4 tsp	chopped fresh oregano (or 1 tsp [5 mL] dried)	20 mL
1 tsp	granulated sugar	5 mL
1/4 tsp	hot pepper flakes	1 mL
12 oz	penne	375 g
	Salt and pepper	

1. In a large saucepan, heat oil over medium-high heat. Add garlic and cook, stirring, for 1 minute. Add ground chicken; cook, breaking it up with a spoon, for 6 minutes or until no longer pink.

2. Stir in tomatoes, wine, parsley, basil, oregano, sugar and hot pepper flakes. Bring to a boil; reduce heat to medium-low, cover and cook for 20 minutes.

3. Meanwhile, in a large pot of boiling salted water, cook penne for 8 to 10 minutes or until tender but firm. Drain, add to the sauce and toss to coat well. Season with salt and pepper to taste.

Chicken Pasta Puttanesca

Cheap and easy — perhaps like the ladies of the night who were supposed to have given their name to a racy pasta sauce — this flavorful pasta is only for those who love zesty food. Serve with an earthy red wine.

MAKE AHEAD

Sauce can be completely made ahead, cooled, covered and refrigerated for up to 1 day. Reheat gently on top of the stove, stirring often.

SHOPPING TIP

Buy boneless breasts or thighs for this dish — whichever are on special at the supermarket.

SUGGESTED MENU

Chicken Pasta
Puttanesca

Crusty Bread

Green Salad

Lemon Ice
and Cookies

3 tbsp	olive oil	45 mL
1 lb	boneless skinless chicken breasts or thighs, cut into 1/2-inch (1 cm) strips	500 g
2	cans (28 oz [796 mL]) Italian plum tomatoes, drained and coarsely chopped	2
1 tsp	dried Italian herb seasoning	5 mL
Pinch	red pepper flakes	Pinch
1/4 cup	drained capers	50 mL
1/2 cup	pitted black olives, chopped	125 mL
4	cloves garlic, chopped	4
1/2 cup	chopped fresh parsley	125 mL
1	can (1 3/4 oz [48 g]) anchovies*, drained and chopped	1
	Salt	
1 lb	spaghetti	500 g
	Additional fresh parsley	

To eliminate some of the salt from the anchovies, drain them and soak them in milk while preparing the other ingredients; then drain again and chop.

1. In a large saucepan, heat oil over medium-high heat. Add chicken and cook, stirring often, for 5 minutes or until no longer pink.

2. Add tomatoes and bring to a boil. Add Italian seasoning, red pepper flakes, capers, black olives, garlic, parsley, anchovies and salt to taste. Reduce heat to medium and cook for 15 minutes or until thickened slightly.

3. Meanwhile, in a large pot of boiling salted water, cook spaghetti for 8 to 10 minutes or until tender but firm. Drain. Divide among pasta bowls or plates. Spoon sauce on top and sprinkle with the additional fresh parsley.

Mediterranean Pasta

Canned artichoke hearts and spaghetti sauce make a fast and delicious addition to this chicken and pasta dish.

MAKE AHEAD

The sauce can be made up to 1 day ahead, covered and refrigerated. Reheat gently, stirring often.

SHOPPING TIP

For convenience, buy chicken pre-cut into stir-fry strips.

SUGGESTED MENU

Mediterranean Pasta

Crusty Bread

Green Salad

Fresh Fruit

4	slices bacon, diced	4
8 oz	skinless boneless chicken breasts, cut into 1/2-inch (1 cm) strips	250 g
1	can (24 oz [680 mL]) meatless pasta sauce, preferably chunky	1
1 tsp	dried rosemary leaves	5 mL
1	can (14 oz [398 mL]) artichoke hearts, drained and quartered	1
1/2 cup	sliced black olives	125 mL
	Salt and pepper	
12 oz	spaghetti or linguine	375 g
	Chopped fresh parsley	
	Crumbled feta cheese	

1. In a large skillet over medium–high heat, cook the bacon, stirring often, for 6 minutes or until almost crisp. Add chicken and cook for 3 minutes or until no longer pink.

2. Stir in pasta sauce and rosemary. Reduce heat to medium-low, cover and cook for 15 minutes, stirring occasionally. Stir in artichoke hearts and olives; cover and cook for 3 minutes or until heated through. Season to taste with salt and pepper.

3. Meanwhile, in a large pot of boiling salted water, cook pasta for 8 to 10 minutes or until tender but firm. Drain. Divide among pasta bowls or plates. Spoon sauce on top and sprinkle with parsley and feta.

Anne Lindsay's Easy Creamy Chicken Fettuccine

My good friend, Anne Lindsay, specializes in making food that is not only healthy but delicious. This great way to use cooked chicken is from her *New Light Cooking* (Ballantine Books). You might like to grate extra Parmesan cheese to pass with the pasta.

SUGGESTED MENU

Easy Creamy Chicken Fettuccine

Crusty Brown Rolls

Green Salad

Strawberries with Frozen Yogurt

8 oz	fettuccine or spaghetti	250 g
2 tsp	olive oil	10 mL
2 cups	sliced mushrooms	500 mL
1 cup	chopped red onions	250 mL
1 cup	sliced celery	250 mL
3	cloves garlic, minced	3
1 cup	2% evaporated milk	250 mL
1 1/2 cups	cooked chicken, cut into strips	375 mL
1/4 cup	chopped fresh parsley	50 mL
1/4 cup	chopped fresh basil*	50 mL
1/4 cup	freshly grated Parmesan cheese	50 mL
	Salt and pepper	

1. In a large pot of boiling salted water, cook fettuccine for 8 to 10 minutes or until tender but firm; drain.

2. Meanwhile, in a large saucepan, heat oil over medium heat. Add mushrooms, onions, celery and garlic; cook, stirring often, for 8 to 10 minutes or until tender.

3. Stir in milk, chicken, parsley, basil, cheese and drained pasta; simmer, stirring gently, for 3 minutes. Season to taste with salt and pepper.

* If fresh basil is not available, substitute 2 tsp (10 mL) dried basil and cook it along with the onions.

Chicken and Pasta with Sun-Dried Tomato Cream

Dry-packed sun-dried tomatoes have a lovely concentrated flavor that makes this pasta sauce quite different from the usual tomato sauce. It's quick and easy company fare. If you have the urge to try it and don't have cooked chicken on hand, merely sauté fresh chicken strips in butter for 5 minutes or until they change color.

MAKE AHEAD

The sauce can be prepared to the end of step 2, cooled, covered and refrigerated for up to 1 day. Bring to a gentle simmer to proceed.

SHOPPING TIPS

Dry-packed sun-dried tomatoes are found in the produce section of the supermarket. They are less expensive than those packed in oil and last well in your cupboard for recipes such as this. They need no pre-soaking for this kind of dish.

1 tbsp	olive oil	15 mL
2	cloves garlic, minced	2
1/2 cup	dry-packed sun-dried tomatoes	125 mL
1 tbsp	tomato paste	15 mL
1 cup	chicken stock	250 mL
1 cup	whipping cream	250 mL
	Salt and pepper	
2 1/2 cups	cooked chicken, cut into strips	625 mL
1/4 cup	chopped fresh parsley	50 mL
1 tsp	dried basil	5 mL
1 tsp	granulated sugar	5 mL
11 oz	package fresh fettuccine (or 12 oz [375 g] dried)	350 g

1. In a large skillet, heat oil over low heat. Add garlic and cook for 30 seconds. Stir in sun-dried tomatoes, tomato paste and stock. Bring to a boil, reduce heat to medium-low and simmer, uncovered, for 10 minutes or until tomatoes are very soft.

2. Transfer tomato mixture to a blender or food processor; purée. Return to skillet. Whisk in cream and bring to a boil; cook, stirring, for 2 to 3 minutes or until thickened. Season to taste with salt and pepper.

3. Stir in chicken, parsley, basil and sugar. Cook for 3 minutes or until heated through.

4. Meanwhile, in a large pot of boiling salted water, cook fresh pasta for 2 to 3 minutes or according to package directions. (Cook dried pasta for 8 to 10 minutes or until tender but firm.) Drain pasta and toss with sauce.

SUGGESTED MENU

Chicken and Pasta with Sun-Dried Tomato Cream

❧

Green Beans

❧

Spinach and Mushroom Salad

❧

Crusty Rolls

❧

Fresh Fruit

Chicken Chili Macaroni

This quick pasta dish, cooked all in one pan, will be a real family pleaser.

VARIATION

For an Italian version, substitute 1 tsp (5 mL) Italian herb seasoning for the chili powder, use Italian-style stewed tomatoes and 1/2 cup (125 mL) Parmesan cheese for the Monterey Jack cheese. Serve with crusty rolls.

SUGGESTED MENU

Chicken Chili Macaroni

Tortilla Chips

Green Salad

Chocolate Pudding
or Rice Pudding

1 lb	lean ground chicken	500 g
1	clove garlic, minced	1
1	can (14 oz [398 mL]) stewed tomatoes, preferably Mexican-style	1
1	can (14 oz [398 mL]) tomato sauce	1
1 tbsp	chili powder	15 mL
1/2 tsp	dried oregano	2 mL
1/2 tsp	ground cumin	2 mL
1 cup	elbow or wagon wheel macaroni	250 mL
1 cup	fresh or frozen cut green beans	250 mL
	Salt and pepper	
1 cup	shredded Monterey Jack *or* Cheddar cheese	250 mL

1. In a large skillet, cook chicken with garlic over medium-high heat, breaking it up with a wooden spoon, for 5 minutes or until chicken is no longer pink.

2. Stir in tomatoes, tomato sauce, chili powder, oregano and cumin. Bring to a boil. Stir in macaroni and green beans; bring back to a boil. Reduce heat to medium-low, cover and cook, stirring occasionally, for 15 minutes or until the pasta and beans are tender. Season to taste with salt and pepper. Serve sprinkled with cheese.

Chicken Primavera

Choose whatever vegetables are in season for this quick and easy supper — sliced asparagus, green beans, snow peas, zucchini or strips of bell pepper.

SHOPPING TIP

For convenience, look for pre-cut broccoli florets in the produce department of the grocery store.

SUGGESTED MENU

Chicken Primavera

Green Salad with
Tomato Wedges

Crusty Bread

Coffee Ice Cream with
Chocolate Sauce

2 tbsp	cornstarch	25 mL
2 cups	chicken stock	500 mL
12 oz	spaghetti *or* linguine	375 g
2	cloves garlic, minced	2
2 cups	broccoli florets	500 mL
2	carrots, sliced	2
1 tsp	dried Italian herb seasoning	5 mL
2 cups	cubed cooked chicken	500 mL
1/2 cup	freshly grated Parmesan cheese	125 mL
	Additional Parmesan cheese	

1. Dissolve cornstarch in 1/4 cup (50 mL) of the stock. Set aside.

2. In a large pot of boiling salted water, cook spaghetti for 8 to 10 minutes or until tender but firm; drain.

3. Meanwhile, in a saucepan combine the remaining stock, garlic, broccoli, carrots and seasoning. Bring to a boil; reduce heat to medium and cook, uncovered, for 3 minutes or until the vegetables are tender-crisp. Stir in cornstarch mixture; cook, stirring, until thickened. Add chicken and cook, stirring for 2 minutes or until heated through.

4. Toss with spaghetti and cheese. Serve with additional cheese for spooning on top.

Spanish Rice and Chicken with Beans

Thighs, instead of boneless breasts, are delicious in this easy one-dish supper. Allow 2 thighs per person and an extra 5 or 10 minutes of cooking time.

MAKE AHEAD

The entire recipe except for the parsley can be made up to 1 day ahead. To reheat, add 1/2 cup (125 mL) water or stock and gently cook on top of the stove without stirring. Stir in parsley to serve.

SUGGESTED MENU

Spanish Rice and
Chicken with Beans

Green Salad

Crusty Bread

Orange and
Grapefruit Slices

1 tbsp	olive oil	15 mL
4	skinless boneless chicken breasts	4
	Salt and pepper	
1	onion, sliced	1
1	large red or green bell pepper, cut into strips	1
2	cloves garlic, minced	2
1 cup	white rice (medium, long-grain or parboiled)	250 mL
1 tsp	ground cumin	5 mL
1/4 tsp	hot pepper flakes	1 mL
2 1/2 cups	chicken stock	625 mL
1	can (5.5 oz [156 mL]) tomato paste	1
1	can (19 oz [540 mL]) white kidney beans, rinsed and drained	1
1/2 cup	chopped fresh parsley	125 mL

1. In a large deep skillet, heat oil over medium heat. Sprinkle chicken with salt and pepper. In batches, cook chicken, turning once, for 4 minutes or until golden on both sides. Transfer to a plate.

2. Pour off all but 1 tbsp (15 mL) of drippings from the pan. Add onion and pepper; cook for 5 minutes or until softened and golden.

3. Add garlic, rice, cumin and hot pepper flakes; cook, stirring, for 1 minute. Stir in stock and tomato paste; bring to a boil. Add beans and chicken (along with any juice); reduce heat to low, cover and cook for about 20 minutes or until chicken is no longer pink inside and the rice is tender. Stir in parsley and serve.

Chicken and Mushroom Risotto

If you have mushrooms on hand, you can turn leftover cooked chicken into a comforting and interesting main course — just the thing for tired, hungry souls.

SHOPPING TIP

Arborio rice is an Italian short-grain rice found in most supermarkets, and it's best for risotto because it is plump and sticky. However, if you can't locate it, try another short-grain or even a medium-grain.

SUGGESTED MENU

Chicken and Mushroom Risotto

Brown Rolls

Green Salad

Lemon Ice

2 tbsp	butter	25 mL
1 tbsp	olive oil	15 mL
8 oz	mushrooms, quartered (about 3 cups [750 mL])	250 g
1	onion, chopped	1
2 tsp	minced fresh thyme (or 1/2 tsp [2 mL] dried)	10 mL
1 cup	arborio rice	250 mL
3 1/2 cups	hot chicken stock (approximate)	875 mL
2 cups	shredded or diced cooked chicken	500 mL
1 cup	frozen green peas	250 mL
1/2 cup	freshly grated Parmesan cheese	125 mL
2 tbsp	chopped fresh chives *or* chopped green onion tops	25 mL
	Salt and pepper	
	Additional Parmesan cheese	

1. In a heavy-bottomed saucepan over medium heat, melt half the butter with the oil. Add mushrooms and cook for 7 minutes or until tender. Remove with a slotted spoon.

2. Melt remaining butter. Add onion and thyme; cook for 5 minutes or until softened. Add rice and cook, stirring, for 1 minute or until coated with butter.

3. Pour in hot stock 1/2 cup (125 mL) at a time, stirring constantly and waiting until stock is mostly absorbed before adding more, all the time keeping the rice at a brisk simmer. (The risotto should always be moist.) After 18 minutes, taste the rice; it should be *al dente* (tender but firm to the bite). You may not need to add all of the stock.

4. Stir in chicken, peas and mushrooms. Cook 2 minutes or until heated through.

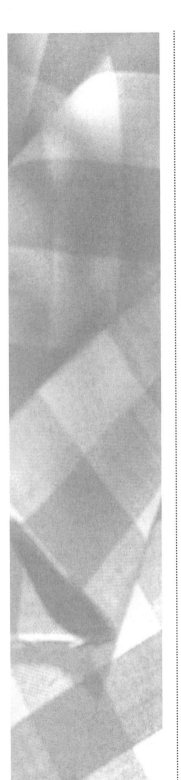

5. Stir in cheese, chives and salt and pepper to taste. Serve immediately in warm shallow bowls with additional cheese for garnish.

Chicken Fried Rice

Since fried rice is best made with cooked rice that's cold, cook extra for supper the night before. This dish is certainly a whole meal in one, and although the recipe looks long, it is very simple to make.

SHOPPING TIP

Different brands of soya sauce have varying amounts of salt; for this recipe, be sure to buy a low-salt sauce. For speedier preparation, look for chicken packaged as stir-fry strips in the supermarket.

SUGGESTED MENU

Chicken Fried Rice

Melon Wedges
Sprinkled with Diced
Ginger in Syrup

1/3 cup	low-salt soya sauce	75 mL
2 tbsp	rice wine *or* dry sherry	25 mL
4	cloves garlic, minced	4
2 tsp	oriental sesame oil	10 mL
12 oz	skinless boneless chicken breasts, cut into 1/4-inch (5 mm) strips	375 g
2 tbsp	vegetable oil (approximate)	25 mL
1	egg, lightly beaten	1
3 tbsp	fermented black beans, rinsed	45 mL
2 tbsp	minced ginger root	25 mL
1	red bell pepper, diced	1
8 oz	snow peas, trimmed and thinly sliced on a diagonal	250 g
4 cups	cold cooked white rice	1 L
4	green onions, sliced	4

1. In a bowl stir together half the soya sauce, half the rice wine, half the garlic and the sesame oil. Add chicken to soya sauce mixture and turn to coat. Set aside.

2. In a small bowl, stir together remaining soya sauce and the wine. Set aside.

3. In a wok or large skillet, heat 1 tbsp (15 mL) of the oil over medium-high heat and swirl it about the pan. Pour in the egg to form a film on the bottom by pushing it about with a fork. When set, remove to a bowl and break up. Wipe out pan and heat half of the remaining oil.

4. Stir-fry chicken mixture for 3 minutes or until it is cooked through. With a slotted spoon, remove to a bowl.

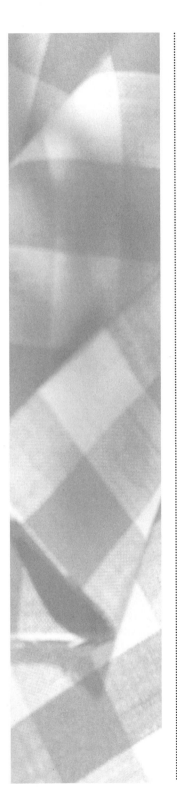

5. Wipe out the pan; heat remaining oil. Add black beans, remaining garlic and ginger; stir-fry for 30 seconds. Add red pepper and stir-fry for 2 minutes or until tender-crisp, adding more oil if necessary. Add snow peas, chicken, rice and green onions; stir-fry for 2 minutes or until heated through. Stir in the remaining soya-wine mixture. Transfer to a heated platter and garnish with the egg.

Great Grills

Gremolata Grilled Chicken

The gremolata mixture is usually a final garnish for veal stew, but it makes a delicious addition to grilled chicken as well. It also works well for boneless chicken breasts.

SUGGESTED MENU

Gremolata Grilled Chicken

Orzo

Sautéed Red Pepper Strips

Green Salad

Cantaloupe Wedges

★ Orzo is a small rice-like pasta that I like to cook in twice the amount of chicken stock instead of in a huge amount of water like other pasta. I then stir in some chopped fresh parsley before serving.

GREASE BARBECUE GRILL AND PREHEAT TO MEDIUM-HIGH

2	cloves garlic, minced	2
2 tbsp	minced fresh parsley	25 mL
1 tbsp	chopped lemon zest	15 mL
2 tbsp	fresh lemon juice	25 mL
1 tbsp	vegetable oil	15 mL
4	boneless chicken thighs	4

1. In a small bowl, combine garlic, parsley and lemon zest. Set aside 1 tbsp (15 mL) of the mixture and combine remainder of the mixture with lemon juice and oil. Press mixture into both sides of the thighs.

2. Grill for about 12 minutes, turning once, until the chicken is no longer pink inside. Sprinkle with the reserved gremolata and serve.

Jalapeno-Glazed Chicken Legs

Pre-cooking chicken legs in the microwave oven makes for a fast barbecued treat. If jalapeno jelly is not available, try redcurrant or apple jelly mixed with a pinch of hot pepper flakes.

SUGGESTED MENU

Jalapeno-Glazed
Chicken Legs

❧

Corn Bread

❧

Coleslaw

❧

★ Black Bean Salad

❧

Chocolate Ice Cream

★ **Black Bean Salad**
Combine a rinsed and drained can of black beans, 2 sliced green onions and 1 diced red bell pepper with a lime vinaigrette made of 1/3 cup (75 mL) vegetable oil, 2 tbsp (25 mL) fresh lime juice, and salt and pepper to taste.

GREASE BARBECUE GRILL AND PREHEAT TO MEDIUM-HIGH
11- BY 7-INCH (2 L) GLASS BAKING DISH

4	chicken legs	4
1/2 cup	jalapeno jelly	125 mL
2 tbsp	butter	25 mL
1 tbsp	fresh lime juice *or* lemon juice	15 mL
	Salt and pepper	

1. In a baking dish, arrange chicken legs skin-side down with the thighs along the outside of the dish and the drumsticks in the center. Cover with waxed paper and microwave on High for 7 minutes per pound, turning over when halfway through. Let stand for 5 minutes.

2. Meanwhile, in a small saucepan, combine jelly and butter. Stir over medium-high heat until melted. Stir in lime juice and set aside.

3. Sprinkle chicken with salt and pepper; place on grill and cook for 3 to 4 minutes, turning once and brushing with the glaze. Cook for another 3 to 4 minutes until crisp and brown.

Chicken-Chutney Kabobs

SERVES 6

A spicy yogurt coating renders the chicken moist and delicious in this interesting dinner-on-a-stick. It's great for family — but could certainly be company fare.

MAKE AHEAD

The chicken can be marinated up to 8 hours ahead in the refrigerator. Bring to room temperature for 30 minutes before cooking.

SHOPPING TIPS

Look for basmati rice (suggested accompaniment) in international grocery stores. It is an aromatic long-grain rice with a nutty taste and worth the extra money it costs. If unavailable, of course, regular or parboiled long-grain rice will certainly do here. Look for poppadums and mango chutney in the international section of your supermarket.

GREASE GRILL AND PREHEAT TO MEDIUM-HIGH

1 cup	mango chutney	250 mL
1/2 cup	plain yogurt	125 mL
1 tsp	ground cumin	5 mL
1/2 tsp	turmeric *or* curry powder	2 mL
1 tbsp	olive oil	15 mL
1	onion, cut into wedges	1
1	red bell pepper, cut into 1-inch (2.5 cm) squares	1
2	small zucchini, cut into 1-inch (2.5 cm) slices	2
1 1/2 lbs	boneless chicken breasts or thighs, cut into 1 1/2–inch (4 cm) pieces	750 g

1. Chop any big pieces in the chutney and combine in a medium-sized bowl with the yogurt, cumin, turmeric and oil. Add the chicken and marinate at room temperature for 30 minutes.

2. Reserving the marinade, thread chicken pieces alternately with onion, red pepper and zucchini onto 6 long skewers. Place on grill (or under the broiler) and cook, turning often and brushing with the marinade, for 15 minutes or until the chicken is no longer pink inside.

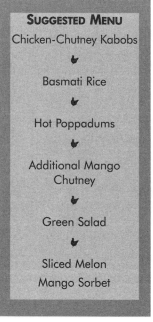

SUGGESTED MENU

Chicken-Chutney Kabobs

☙

Basmati Rice

☙

Hot Poppadums

☙

Additional Mango Chutney

☙

Green Salad

☙

Sliced Melon Mango Sorbet

Grilled Chicken Satay with Coconut-Peanut Sauce

These easy skewers, with their interesting sauce, are fun to serve for a party — alone or as part of a mixed grill.

If using wooden skewers, soak in cold water for 20 to 30 minutes

MAKE AHEAD

The chicken strips can be marinated, covered and refrigerated, up to 8 hours ahead. Bring to room temperature 30 minutes before cooking. The dipping sauce can be made, covered and refrigerated up to 1 day ahead.

SHOPPING TIP

For convenience, buy pre-cut stir-fry strips for the satay.

SUGGESTED MENU

Grilled Chicken Satay with Coconut-Peanut Sauce

Rice

Green Beans

Fresh Fruit Salad

GREASE BARBECUE GRILL AND PREHEAT TO MEDIUM-HIGH

1 lb	skinless boneless chicken breasts, cut into 1/2-inch (1 cm) strips	500 g
2 tbsp	fresh lime juice	25 mL
2 tbsp	oriental sesame oil	25 mL
1 tsp	curry powder	5 mL

COCONUT-PEANUT SAUCE

1/3 cup	peanut butter	75 mL
1/4 cup	sweetened flaked coconut	50 mL
1	clove garlic, chopped	1
1/4 cup	fresh lime juice	50 mL
2 tbsp	low-salt soya sauce	25 mL
1/3 cup	fresh coriander sprigs (optional)	75 mL

1. In a glass bowl, combine chicken with lime juice, sesame oil and curry powder. Set aside for 15 minutes at room temperature.

2. Coconut-Peanut Sauce: While chicken marinates, combine in a blender the peanut butter, coconut, garlic, lime juice, soya sauce and coriander (if using); blend until smooth. Transfer to a bowl and refrigerate if making ahead.

3. Reserving the marinade, weave chicken strips onto skewers; place on grill and cook, basting with the marinade, for about 4 minutes a side or until the chicken is no longer pink inside. Serve with coconut-peanut sauce.

Grilled Chicken Breasts with Warm Potato and Portobello Salad

SERVES 4

A simple warm salad of potatoes and barbecued mushrooms is accompanied by succulent grilled chicken breasts for an easy-but-impressive company meal.

LARGE PIECE OF BARBECUE FOIL, GREASED OR SPRAYED WITH BAKING SPRAY
GREASE BARBECUE GRILL AND PREHEAT TO MEDIUM-HIGH

4	unpeeled new potatoes, sliced 1/8 inch (3 mm) thick	4
2	cloves garlic, sliced	2
	Olive oil	
1/2 tsp	paprika	2 mL
	Salt and pepper	
2 tbsp	white wine vinegar	25 mL
2 tsp	Dijon mustard	10 mL
4	skinless boneless chicken breasts	4
4	portobello mushrooms	4
1/4 cup	chopped fresh parsley	50 mL

1. Arrange potato slices on prepared foil and spread them out in a thin layer. Add garlic, drizzle with 1 tbsp (15 mL) olive oil and sprinkle with paprika, 1/2 tsp (2 mL) salt and 1/4 tsp (1 mL) pepper. Wrap potatoes securely in the foil; place on the grill and cook for 30 minutes, turning occasionally, until the potatoes are soft.

2. Meanwhile, whisk together 1/3 cup (75 mL) olive oil, vinegar, mustard, and salt and pepper to taste. Pour half of the mixture (reserving the remainder for use in Step 3) into a shallow baking dish. Add chicken breasts and mushrooms and turn to coat well with the mixture, brushing the mixture inside the mushroom caps. Place chicken on grill and cook, turning once, for 12 to 15 minutes or until chicken is no longer pink inside. Place mushrooms on grill and cook for 5 to 7 minutes, turning once.

Recipe continues...

CHICKEN BURGERS WITH KIWI SALSA (PAGE 165) ➤

SUGGESTED MENU

Grilled Chicken Breasts
with Warm Potato and
Portobello Salad

❧

Green Salad

❧

★ Basil Sliced Tomatoes

❧

Grilled Peach Halves
with Vanilla Ice Cream

★ Basil Sliced Tomatoes
*Drizzle sliced tomatoes with
balsamic vinegar and
sprinkle with slivered
fresh basil.*

3. Slice the mushrooms and place in a large bowl with the cooked potatoes and parsley. Pour reserved oil mixture over top and gently toss to coat. Serve warm with chicken breasts.

◄ PESTO-GRILLED CHICKEN WITH FRESH TOMATO PASTA (PAGE 170)

Thai-Grilled Chicken

SERVES 4

If you wish, you can use 8 boneless thighs instead of the breasts for this fresh-tasting grilled chicken.

MAKE AHEAD

The chicken can be rubbed with the basil mixture, covered and refrigerated for up to 8 hours ahead. Bring to room temperature for 30 minutes before cooking.

SUGGESTED MENU

Thai-Grilled Chicken

★ Thai Noodle Salad

Steamed Pea Pods
(snow peas or
sugar snap)

Coconut Ice Cream or
Mango Sorbet

★ *Thai Noodle Salad*
Use the recipe for Thai Chicken-Noodle Salad (see page 69) leaving out the cooked chicken.

GREASE BARBECUE GRILL AND PREHEAT TO MEDIUM-HIGH

1/3 cup	packed fresh basil leaves	75 mL
1/3 cup	packed coriander leaves	75 mL
1 tbsp	chopped ginger root	15 mL
2	cloves garlic	2
1 tbsp	soya sauce	15 mL
1 tbsp	Thai fish sauce	15 mL
1 tbsp	vegetable oil	15 mL
1 tbsp	packed brown sugar	15 mL
1 tbsp	fresh lime juice *or* lemon juice	15 mL
1/4 tsp	hot pepper flakes	1 mL
4	skinless boneless chicken breasts	4

1. In a blender or small food processor, combine basil, coriander, ginger, garlic, soya sauce, fish sauce, oil, brown sugar, lime juice and hot pepper flakes; process until well blended. Measure out 2 tbsp (25 mL) of mixture and set aside.

2. Place chicken in a single layer in a glass dish; rub thoroughly with remaining basil mixture. Cover and let sit at room temperature for 30 minutes.

3. Place chicken on grill and cook, turning once, for 5 minutes a side or until no longer pink inside. To serve, thinly slice each breast crosswise on a diagonal and drizzle with the reserved basil mixture.

Mustard-Thyme Grilled Breasts

With only a handful of ingredients, this marinade keeps the bone-in breasts moist and delicious.

MAKE AHEAD

The chicken can be marinated, covered and refrigerated for up to 4 hours ahead. Bring to room temperature for 30 minutes before cooking.

SUGGESTED MENU

Mustard-Thyme Grilled Breasts

♥

Buttered New Potatoes

♥

Grilled Tomato Halves

♥

Green Beans

♥

Blueberries and Honeyed Yogurt

GREASE BARBECUE GRILL AND PREHEAT TO MEDIUM-HIGH

1/3 cup	Dijon mustard	75 mL
1 tbsp	vegetable oil	15 mL
1 tbsp	white wine vinegar	15 mL
1 tsp	cayenne pepper	5 mL
1 tsp	dried thyme	5 mL
4	skin-on bone-in chicken breasts	4

1. In a bowl combine half the mustard, the oil, vinegar, half the cayenne and half the thyme. Place chicken in a glass dish and spread mixture over the breasts. Cover and let sit for 15 to 30 minutes at room temperature. In a small bowl, stir together the remaining mustard, cayenne and thyme and set aside.

2. Place chicken, skin-side down on the grill and cook for 15 minutes, turning often.

3. Turn the chicken skin-side up and brush with the reserved mustard mixture. Cook for 10 to 15 minutes longer or until the chicken is no longer pink inside.

Honey-Dijon Grilled Thighs

You can easily substitute 4 skinless boneless breasts for the thighs in this fast and easy grilled chicken recipe.

SUGGESTED MENU

Honey-Dijon Grilled Thighs

★ Tiny New Potato Skewers

★ Green Salad with Garlic Vinaigrette

Fresh Fruit

★ *Tiny New Potato Skewers*
See page 172.

★ *Green Salad with Garlic Vinaigrette*
Toss 8 cups (2 L) mixed torn salad greens with a dressing of 1/4 cup (50 mL) olive oil, 1 tbsp (15 mL) red or white wine vinegar, 1 clove garlic mashed with salt and black pepper to taste.

GREASE BARBECUE GRILL AND PREHEAT TO MEDIUM-HIGH

3 tbsp	Dijon mustard	45 mL
2 tbsp	liquid honey	25 mL
1 tbsp	vegetable oil	15 mL
1 tbsp	fresh lemon juice	15 mL
1 tsp	dried thyme	5 mL
8	boneless chicken thighs	8
	Salt and pepper	

1. In a bowl combine mustard, honey, oil, lemon juice and thyme.
2. Sprinkle chicken thighs with salt and pepper. Grill for 5 minutes; turn and grill for another 5 to 6 minutes or until the chicken is no longer pink inside. Brush with mustard mixture during the last minute of cooking.

Chicken Burgers with Kiwi Salsa

GREASE BARBECUE GRILL AND PREHEAT TO MEDIUM-HIGH

1	egg	1
1 1/4 lbs	ground chicken	625 g
1/3 cup	dry bread crumbs	75 mL
3 tbsp	milk *or* cream	45 mL
1/2 tsp	salt	2 mL
1/4 tsp	pepper	1 mL
6	toasted hamburger buns	6

1. In a bowl, beat the egg; mix in the chicken, bread crumbs, milk, salt and pepper. Form into 6 patties, about 3/4 inch (2 cm) thick.

2. Place on grill and cook, turning once, for 10 minutes or until chicken is no longer pink inside. Place in buns; spoon on KIWI SALSA (recipe follows, next page).

(recipe follows, next page)

SERVES 6

MAKE AHEAD

The burgers can be formed, covered and refrigerated for up to 6 hours ahead. The Kiwi Salsa can be made a couple of hours ahead, covered and refrigerated.

SHOPPING TIPS

Look for buns other than plain hamburger buns. For a change, try kaiser rolls, focaccia or pita breads. Buns always taste better warm or toasted and you can do this right on the grill.

SUGGESTED MENU

Chicken Burgers with Kiwi Salsa

Pasta Salad

Sliced Tomatoes

Chocolate Sundaes

Kiwi Salsa

This freshly made salsa livens up burgers, but they're also delicious with store-bought salsa or your favorite relish.

2	kiwi fruit, peeled and diced	2
1/2 cup	diced red onions	125 mL
2 tbsp	fresh lime juice	25 mL
2 tsp	packed brown sugar	10 mL
1/2 tsp	dried oregano	2 mL

1. In a small bowl, stir together the kiwi fruit, onions, lime juice, sugar and oregano.

Caesar Burgers

Everyone will love the flavors of their favorite salad in these juicy burgers.

SUGGESTED MENU
Caesar Burgers

Chocolate Brownies

GREASE BARBECUE GRILL AND PREHEAT TO MEDIUM-HIGH

1	egg	1
1 1/4 lbs	ground chicken	625 g
1/4 cup	freshly grated Parmesan cheese	50 mL
2 tbsp	fresh lemon juice	25 mL
1 tbsp	anchovy paste	15 mL
1 tbsp	Worcestershire sauce	15 mL
1/4 tsp	pepper	1 mL
2 tbsp	olive oil	25 mL
1	clove garlic, minced	1
4	kaiser rolls, halved	4
4	leaves romaine lettuce	4

1. In a bowl, beat the egg; mix in the chicken, half the Parmesan cheese, the lemon juice, anchovy paste, Worcestershire sauce and pepper. Shape into 4 patties, about 3/4 inch (2 cm) thick.

2. Place on grill; cook, turning once, for 10 to 12 minutes or until chicken is no longer pink inside.

3. Meanwhile, combine the oil and garlic and brush over the cut side of the rolls. Place on the grill and toast.

4. Place burgers on rolls; sprinkle with remaining Parmesan cheese and top with romaine lettuce.

Feta Cheese Burgers

Serve these juicy burgers, inspired by Middle Eastern flavors, in warm pita breads.

SUGGESTED MENU

Feta Cheese Burgers

★ Spiced Yogurt

Sliced Tomatoes

★ Cucumber and Onion Salad

Fresh Fruit

★ *Spiced Yogurt*
Whisk together 1/2 cup (125 mL) thick plain yogurt, 1/2 tsp (2 mL) each paprika and cumin, and a pinch of cayenne.

★ *Cucumber and Onion Salad*
Toss sliced cucumbers and onions with salt, pepper and white wine vinegar.

GREASE BARBECUE GRILL AND PREHEAT TO MEDIUM-HIGH

1 1/2 lbs	lean ground chicken	750 g
1/2 tsp	salt	2 mL
1/4 tsp	pepper	1 mL
1/4 tsp	ground cumin	1 mL
2 oz	feta cheese	50 g
2 tbsp	chopped fresh mint (or 2 tsp [10 mL] dried)	25 mL

1. In a bowl combine chicken, salt, pepper and cumin. Divide mixture into 4 portions. Cut cheese into 4 cubes; flatten the cubes and sprinkle with mint. Form 4 chicken patties with the cheese and mint buried in the center of each patty.

2. Place patties on grill; cook, turning once, for 12 to 14 minutes or until patties are no longer pink inside.

Chicken and Summer Fruit Kabobs

For this easy dinner-on-a-stick, you could use melon cubes, quartered peaches, apricot halves or a combination.

MAKE AHEAD

Chicken and fruit can be marinated up to 8 hours ahead in the refrigerator. Bring to room temperature 30 minutes before cooking.

SUGGESTED MENU

Chicken and Summer Fruit Kabobs

Green Salad

Potato Salad

Ice Cream and Cake

GREASE BARBECUE GRILL AND PREHEAT TO MEDIUM

1/4 cup	fresh lime juice *or* lemon juice	50 mL
2 tbsp	vegetable oil	25 mL
1 tbsp	minced ginger root	15 mL
4	skinless boneless chicken breasts	4
4	nectarines, pitted	4
	Salt and pepper	

1. In a bowl combine lime juice, oil and ginger.
2. Cut each chicken breast into 4 large chunks. Quarter the nectarines. Add both to the lime mixture and toss to coat well. Cover and marinate for 30 minutes at room temperature.
3. Reserving the marinade, thread chicken chunks onto skewers; sprinkle with salt and pepper. Place skewers on grill; cover and cook for 10 minutes, brushing with the marinade. Turn and cook for 7 to 12 minutes longer or until the chicken is no longer pink inside.
4. Meanwhile, thread nectarines onto skewers. Place on grill and cook for 5 to 7 minutes, turning once.

Pesto-Grilled Chicken with Fresh Tomato Pasta

A small amount of pesto sauce pushed under the skin of chicken breasts not only gives them a lovely flavor, but helps to keep them moist while they cook.

MAKE AHEAD

The chicken breasts can be prepared, covered and refrigerated up to 8 hours ahead. Bring to room temperature 30 minutes before cooking. The tomato sauce can be made up to 1 hour ahead and left at room temperature.

SUGGESTED MENU

Pesto-Grilled Chicken
with Fresh Tomato Pasta

Crusty Bread

Green Salad

🍃

★ Grilled Peach Halves

★ *Grilled Peach Halves*
Brush peach halves with melted butter, sprinkle with sugar and cinnamon; place on the cool part of the grill to heat through for about 5 to 8 minutes.

GREASE BARBECUE GRILL AND PREHEAT TO MEDIUM-HIGH

4	bone-in skin-on chicken breasts	4
1/2 cup	pesto sauce	125 mL

FRESH TOMATO PASTA

4 cups	corkscrew pasta (or 12 oz [375 g] fettuccine)	1 L
1 tbsp	olive oil	15 mL
4	ripe tomatoes, unpeeled	4
Half	red onion, coarsely chopped	Half
2	cloves garlic, minced	2
2 tbsp	chopped fresh basil (or 1 tsp [5 mL] dried)	25 mL
2 tbsp	chopped fresh oregano (or 1 tsp [5 mL] dried)	25 mL
2 tsp	red wine vinegar	10 mL
1 tsp	packed brown sugar	5 mL
	Salt and pepper	

1. Gently poke your fingers under the skin of each breast and lift the skin slightly. (Be careful not to tear the membrane that connects the skin to the chicken.) Gently stuff 2 tbsp (25 mL) pesto in each breast, massaging to even out.

2. Starting with the pesto-side up, grill chicken for 5 minutes. Turn the breasts and grill for another 5 minutes. Turn again and finish on the grill with the pesto side up for 5 to 7 minutes or until the chicken is no longer pink inside.

3. Fresh Tomato Pasta: Meanwhile, in a large pot of boiling salted water, cook the pasta until tender but firm. Drain well and toss with the oil.

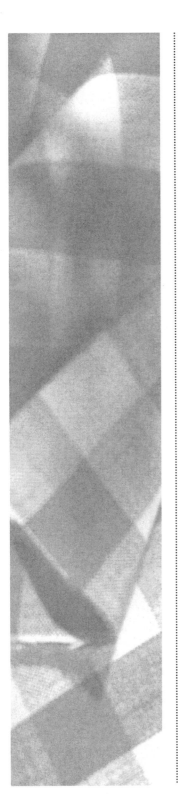

4. While the pasta cooks, core the tomatoes and coarsely chop. In a bowl combine tomatoes, onion, garlic, basil, oregano, vinegar and sugar. Add salt and pepper to taste. Toss with the pasta and serve immediately.

Honey-Sage Grilled Chicken

SERVES 4

For an easy, fun supper, you can make these simple grilled breasts into hearty sandwiches. Slice each breast in half lengthwise and combine the chicken with mayonnaise and grilled red peppers on slices of focaccia.

MAKE AHEAD

The chicken can be marinated, covered and refrigerated for up to 4 hours ahead. Bring to room temperature 30 minutes before cooking.

GREASE BARBECUE GRILL AND PREHEAT TO MEDIUM-HIGH

4	skinless boneless chicken breasts	4
1/4 cup	fresh lemon juice	50 mL
2 tbsp	olive oil	25 mL
1 tbsp	liquid honey	15 mL
2 tsp	dried sage	10 mL
Dash	Tabasco sauce	Dash

1. Place chicken breasts between 2 pieces of plastic wrap and pound to an even 1/2-inch (1 cm) thickness.

2. In a large shallow glass dish, combine the lemon juice, oil, honey, sage and Tabasco sauce. Add chicken and turn to coat well; let stand for 15 minutes.

3. Reserving the marinade, place chicken on grill and cook for about 4 to 5 minutes a side, brushing often with the marinade up to the last 3 minutes.

★ *Tiny New Potato Skewers*
Parboil scrubbed new potatoes for 10 minutes; toss in olive oil, paprika, salt and pepper. Thread onto skewers and grill for about 4 minutes, turning often, until the skins are crisp.

★ *Grilled Nectarine Halves*
Brush pitted nectarine halves with melted butter and lemon juice. Sprinkle with granulated sugar and place on the cool part of the grill for 5 to 7 minutes or until the sugar bubbles and the nectarine halves are warm throughout.

SUGGESTED MENU

Honey-Sage Grilled Chicken

❧

Grilled Red Peppers and Zucchini

❧

★ Tiny New Potato Skewers

❧

★ Grilled Nectarine Halves

Citrus Grilled Chicken Breasts with Yogurt Sauce

The refreshing sauce is just right with this lively grilled chicken.

MAKE AHEAD

The chicken breasts can be marinated up to 24 hours ahead in the refrigerator. Bring to room temperature 30 minutes before cooking.

SUGGESTED MENU

Citrus Grilled Chicken Breasts with Yogurt Sauce

★ Grilled Vegetable Kabobs

Rice

🐦

Cantaloupe Wedges

★ *Grilled Vegetable Kabobs*

Toss eggplant cubes, red pepper pieces, mushrooms and onion wedges in olive oil and minced garlic; thread onto skewers, sprinkle with salt and pepper and grill along with chicken for about 10 minutes, or until tender, turning often.

GREASE BARBECUE GRILL AND PREHEAT TO MEDIUM-HIGH

1 tbsp	grated orange zest	15 mL
1 tbsp	grated lime zest	15 mL
1/4 cup	fresh orange juice	50 mL
1/4 cup	fresh lime juice	50 mL
2 tbsp	olive oil	25 mL
1	fresh jalapeno pepper, seeded and minced	1
4	chicken breasts, patted dry	4

YOGURT SAUCE

1 cup	plain yogurt	250 mL
1	shallot or small onion, finely diced	1
1 tsp	grated orange zest	5 mL
1 tsp	grated lime zest	5 mL
2 tbsp	fresh orange juice	25 mL
2 tbsp	chopped fresh coriander	25 mL
1 tbsp	fresh lime juice	15 mL
	Salt and pepper	

1. In a shallow dish or a sturdy plastic bag, combine orange and lime zest, orange juice, lime juice, olive oil and jalapeno pepper. Add chicken breasts and marinate for 30 minutes at room temperature.

2. Reserving the marinade, place chicken on grill and cook for 7 to 8 minutes a side, turning once and basting with the marinade, until the chicken is no longer pink inside.

3. Yogurt Sauce: Meanwhile, in a small bowl, stir together the yogurt, shallot, zest, orange juice, coriander, lime juice, and salt and pepper to taste. Cover and refrigerate. Serve the hot chicken with the cold sauce.

A simple rub adds lots of flavor and interest to these grilled chicken breasts.

SUGGESTED MENU

Spice-Rubbed
Barbecued Breasts

🐦

Potato Salad

🐦

Corn on the Cob

🐦

★ Tomato Basil Salad

🐦

★ Grilled Nectarines

★ Tomato Basil Salad
Sprinkle sliced tomatoes with snipped fresh basil, salt and pepper; drizzle with balsamic vinegar.

★ Grilled Nectarines
Brush nectarine halves with melted butter, sprinkle with sugar and grill for about 5 minutes or until warm.

Spice-Rubbed Barbecued Breasts

GREASE BARBECUE GRILL AND PREHEAT TO MEDIUM-HIGH

1 tbsp	vegetable oil	15 mL
2	cloves garlic, minced	2
2 tbsp	sweet paprika	25 mL
1 tsp	black pepper	5 mL
1 tsp	chili powder	5 mL
1 tsp	cumin	5 mL
1 tsp	brown sugar	5 mL
1/2 tsp	cayenne pepper	2 mL
1/2 tsp	salt	2 mL
4	skinless boneless chicken breasts	4

1. In a bowl combine oil, garlic, paprika, black pepper, chili powder, cumin, brown sugar, cayenne and salt. Rub mixture all over chicken breasts. Grill, turning once, for 12 to 15 minutes or until chicken is no longer pink inside.

The flavors of your favorite stir-fry are spooned over grilled breasts for an easy sauce.

SUGGESTED MENU

Grilled Chinese Chicken Breasts

♦

Rice and Grilled Vegetable Kabobs or Green Peas

♦

Gingered Melon Wedges

Grilled Chinese Chicken Breasts

GREASE BARBECUE GRILL AND PREHEAT TO MEDIUM-HIGH

4	skinless boneless chicken breasts	4
1 tbsp	sesame oil	15 mL
	Salt and pepper	
3 tbsp	low-salt soya sauce	45 mL
3 tbsp	dry sherry	45 mL
1 tbsp	minced ginger root	15 mL
1 tbsp	honey	15 mL
1	clove garlic, minced	1
1	green onion, sliced	1
1/2 tsp	cornstarch	2 mL
2 tbsp	sesame seeds (optional)	25 mL

1. Place chicken breasts between 2 pieces of plastic wrap and pound with a mallet or rolling pin to an even 1/4-inch (5 mm) thickness. Rub with sesame oil; sprinkle with salt and pepper. Grill for about 4 to 5 minutes per side or until no longer pink inside.

2. Meanwhile, in a small saucepan, combine soya sauce, sherry, ginger, honey, garlic, green onion and cornstarch. Bring to a boil; cook, stirring, until thickened. Spoon sauce over hot chicken and sprinkle with sesame seeds, if using.

Grilled Whole Chicken with Lime or Lemon Butter

This may not be an under-30-minute recipe, but it's a good way to have chicken on hand for speedy recipes such as salads, soups and the like throughout the week. Grill 2 chickens — one to enjoy on Sunday and the other one for leftovers. Or grill one while you have the barbecue on for something else.

GREASE BARBECUE GRILL AND PREHEAT TO MEDIUM-HIGH

1	chicken (about 4 lbs [2 kg]), patted dry	1
1	lime or lemon, halved	1
1 tsp	dried thyme	5 mL
1/4 cup	butter, softened	50 mL
1 tsp	grated lime or lemon zest	5 mL
1/4 cup	fresh lime or lemon juice	50 mL

1. Rub chicken all over, inside and out, with cut side of lime. Sprinkle with thyme.

2. Place chicken, breast-side up, on grill; cook, turning often, for 10 to 15 minutes or until browned. Turn off one burner and place the chicken over the turned-off burner. Increase heat to high on remaining burner; cook, covered, for 1 hour, turning halfway through.

3. Meanwhile, whisk together the butter, lime zest and juice. Brush chicken with mixture. Cook, turning and basting occasionally, for 30 minutes to 1 hour longer or until meat thermometer registers 185° F (85° C).

Teriyaki Chicken with Fresh Peach-Mint Salsa

GREASE BARBECUE GRILL AND PREHEAT TO MEDIUM-HIGH

2 tbsp	soya sauce	25 mL
2 tbsp	rice wine *or* sherry	25 mL
1 tbsp	granulated sugar	15 mL
1 tbsp	minced ginger root	15 mL
2	cloves garlic, crushed	2
4	skinless boneless chicken breasts	4

FRESH PEACH-MINT SALSA

3	peaches, pitted and diced	3
2 tbsp	rice wine vinegar	25 mL
2 tbsp	fresh mint (or 2 tsp [10 mL] dried)	25 mL
1	green onion, sliced	1
1	jalapeno pepper, minced	1
	Salt and pepper	

1. In a sturdy plastic bag or glass dish, combine soya sauce, wine, sugar, ginger and garlic. Add chicken and turn to coat. Close the bag (or cover dish); leave at room temperature for 20 minutes.

2. Fresh Peach-Mint Salsa: Meanwhile, in a small bowl, mix together the peaches, vinegar, mint, green onion and jalapeno pepper. Season to taste with salt and pepper.

3. Grill or broil the chicken, turning once, for about 12 to 15 minutes or until the chicken is no longer pink inside. Serve hot with the salsa.

◂ Full Index ▸

Chicken Index

Chicken Breasts

Chicken Legs

Chicken Wings

Cooked Chicken